SHARING

Jesus

IS EVERYTHING

Also by Alejandro Bullón

The Invitation

The Invitation (Sharing Edition)

SHARING
Jesus
IS EVERYTHING

ALEJANDRO BULLÓN

Pacific Press® Publishing Association
Nampa, Idaho
Oshawa, Ontario, Canada
www.pacificpress.com

Cover design by Steve Lanto
Cover design resources by Lars Justinen © Pacific Press® Publishing Association
Inside design by Aaron Troia

Scriptures quotations are from The New King James Version, copyright ©
1979, 1980, 1982, Thomas Nelson, Inc., Publishers.

The author assumes full responsibility for the accuracy of all facts and
quotations as cited in this book.

You can obtain additional copies of this book by calling toll-free 1-800-
765-6955 or by visiting http://www.adventistbookcenter.com.

Library of Congress Cataloging-in-Publication Data:

Bullon, Alejandro, 1947-
  [Compartir a Jesús es todo. English]
  Sharing Jesus is everything / Alejandro Bullon.
      p. cm.
  English translation of : Compartir a Jesús es todo.
  ISBN 13: 978-0-8163-2419-4 (pbk.)
  ISBN 10: 0-8163-2419-0
  1. Witness bearing (Christianity)—Seventh-day Adventists. I. Title.
  BX6154.B8613 2010
  248'.5—dc22

                                                          2010030837

‘

10 11 12 13 14 • 5 4 3 2 1

Contents

Foreword

"What moves me to write this book is the danger that we face of misunderstanding what the kingdom of God is. That was the tragedy of the disciples, and it could be ours as well." So writes the author of this book.

The question of what comprises the kingdom of God lies at the crux of this work. It is a pressing one for God's people, who are living in the time of the end of earth's history. This question, and the answers that Pastor Alejandro Bullón gives, flow like a river through each chapter.

The kingdom of God on earth has institutions that require statistics, budgets, graphs, and bookkeeping, but it is so much more than that. The worst thing that could happen is for us to start thinking that the divine kingdom is tied directly to growth in membership and that in order to grow it, expand its membership, and increase its net worth, we must ask clever strategists to come up with ever more innovative plans. But the kingdom isn't built on earthly methods and the know-how of talented business people. It has nothing whatsoever to do with human power plays. Any skilled CEO can make the structure grow—that wouldn't require the intervention of the Holy Spirit.

But building this kind of growth isn't the challenge God has given the church. Instead, He wants the church to facilitate spiritual growth in the life of each and every Christian. To all who have received Christ in their hearts, the Lord offers the blessing of coparticipation in the great task of preparing a glorious church that reflects the glory of God. This is the mission that He has entrusted to each of us as believers, and His greatest longing is that we become coworkers with Him in fulfilling it.

If the glory of God is His character, as Ellen White declares, to reflect that glory we must love—because God is love. We must love God and love all of those for whom Christ gave His life. And if we love other people, we will lead them to the Master's feet as Andrew did his brother Peter. This work is indispensable to our spiritual growth.

In this book, Pastor Alejandro Bullón teaches us how easy it is to *share Jesus*. He challenges us to find joy and deep personal satisfaction through witnessing. When you have read this book, you will understand why *sharing Jesus* is so beautiful. *Sharing Him* is what evangelism is all about, and it is what builds the church of God's dream, which is being glorified here on earth in anticipation of its encounter with Him at the Second Coming. God has called all of us to this destiny.

THE EDITORS

Chapter 1

What Kingdom Are We Building?

From habit, my feet follow the path while thoughts whirl through my mind. Oblivious to the lovely evening, I barely notice the glow from the full moon. From my jumbled thoughts, I want to articulate so many things; I long to reach beyond my limited human understanding of spiritual things and the hardness of my own heart. The rhythm of my steps brings to mind Jesus' walks with His uncomprehending disciples. I cringe with shame. I am no different from the disciples! Two thousand years later, I stand here, no wiser than any of the Twelve.

* * * * *

Jesus' repeated attempts to communicate spiritual truths to His disciples met with failure. They nodded as if comprehending. He used familiar vocabulary, but somehow, they repeatedly missed His meaning. It was almost as if Jesus were broadcasting in one frequency, and the disciples were tuned to a different one. The Master would speak of spiritual things, but his listeners, hampered by human teaching or expectations, would, instead, arrive at some conclusion related to daily life or material concerns.

Think of that midnight interview between Nicodemus and the Master. Jesus brought up the topic of new birth. Jesus minced no words; He launched directly into a discussion of spiritual rebirth—conversion. Every person needs a conversion experience in order to live the Christian life, but Nicodemus puzzled over Jesus' choice of words. He blurted out, "How can a man be born when he is old? Can he enter a second time into his mother's womb and be born?" (John 3:4). Nicodemus was highly educated, a spiritual leader among God's chosen people; nevertheless, he completely missed the spiritual intent of what Jesus tried to tell him.

Some time later, the Master sat by a village well where He began a conversation about the water of life with a startled Samaritan woman. Jesus told her about an amazing grace that is capable of quenching spiritual thirst in parched human souls, but she, too, failed to grasp the spiritual meaning. She quipped in response, "Sir, You have nothing to draw with, and the well is deep. Where then do You get that living water?" (John 4:11). He talked about Heaven's refreshment, and she was thinking of well water. How tragic!

Mark 8 includes yet another story illustrating the difficulty human beings have in catching on to spiritual things: "Now the disciples had forgotten to take bread, and they did not have more than one loaf with them in the boat. Then He charged them, saying, 'Take heed, beware of the leaven of the Pharisees and the leaven of Herod.' And they reasoned among themselves, saying, 'It is because we have no bread' " (Mark 8:14–16). The disciples' response is almost humorous. Their viewpoint was again limited to the human and material.

Jesus came to this world to establish His spiritual kingdom; not once did He promote an earthly kingdom. John had announced His coming to establish a spiritual kingdom: "In those days John the Baptist came preaching in the wilderness of Judea, and saying, 'Repent, for the kingdom of heaven is at hand!' " (Matthew 3:1, 2). As predicted, Jesus also spoke of the spiritual nature of His kingdom—126 times in the four Gospels. None of these references included the slightest reason for the disciples to think He referred to an earthly kingdom. His message was made clear by illustrating His spiritual kingdom in terms such as salt, light, yeast, and mustard seed.

But the disciples seemed unable to modify their preconceptions that the Messiah would be a warrior who would defeat the Roman legions and restore Israel as an independent nation. When the disciples visualized the kingdom of heaven, they did so according to human expectations. In their desire for an earthly kingdom, they overlooked the term *heaven* as Jesus taught about the "kingdom of heaven." How ironic that the disciples could talk about the "kingdom of heaven" while simultaneously campaigning for a position of power in the new kingdom.

Throughout His three years of ministry on earth, Jesus repeatedly attempted to teach the disciples about the spiritual nature of His kingdom. Unfortunately, right up to the end, they were still self-deluded. That's why Jesus' crucifixion left them disillusioned, feeling defeated and abandoned.

The Sunday evening following the Crucifixion, while two disciples were walking home to Emmaus, their hopes shattered, one of them, Cleopas, commented to the Stranger who had caught up with them: " 'Are You the only stranger in Jerusalem, and have You not known the things which happened there in these days?' And He said to them, 'What things?' So they said to Him, 'The things concerning Jesus of Nazareth, who was a Prophet mighty in deed and word before God and all the people, and how the chief priests and our rulers delivered Him to be condemned to death, and crucified Him. But we were hoping that it was He who was going to redeem Israel' " (Luke 24:18–21).

Why were Cleopas's words so pessimistic? "We had hoped that He would be the Redeemer of Israel," he lamented. The dejected disciples had completely failed to grasp the meaning of the kingdom Jesus came to establish. They were unaware that the betrayal and sufferings Jesus willingly endured, and His death on the cross, were necessary to enable the promised redemption. They concluded that Jesus had simply let them down. It's hard to imagine anyone failing a final exam more miserably than those students of the Master.

Praise God, Jesus never forsakes those who fail. He is the God of second chances, always ready to write on a blank page. That same Sunday evening He appeared to His disciples, who were cowering behind locked doors, fearful that they, too, would face betrayal and suffering. Suddenly, Jesus was among them, calming their fears, lifting their depression, and challenging them to begin building His kingdom.

What kingdom could they possibly build now if during three years with the Master Teacher they had learned so little? In His compassion, Jesus gave the disciples a second chance, an accelerated remedial class; He remained with them for an additional forty days to clarify the spiritual nature of His kingdom. Luke describes these forty days: "He also presented Himself alive after His suffering by many infallible proofs, being seen by them during forty days and speaking of the things pertaining to the kingdom of God" (Acts 1:3).

The kingdom of God had been the central theme of Jesus' ministry during the previous three years. But the Twelve had learned so little. Now resurrected, waiting to return to heaven, Jesus graciously remained with the Eleven these additional forty days, and once again He emphasized the very same theme—the kingdom of God. But wait; He had additional instruction for the disciples: don't leave Jerusalem. You must wait right here for the promised Holy Spirit. Why would He give such command? Because the kingdom of God is a spiritual kingdom and it can be built only under the guiding hand of the Spirit.

To compare the two kingdoms (the earthly kingdom for which the disciples hoped, and the spiritual kingdom that He was promoting), Jesus used the example of two baptisms to help His followers picture the difference. Consider the baptism practiced by John, immersion in water—a visible act. In modern baptisms, family and friends gather as witnesses, taking photos and celebrating the occasion. Candidates' names are recorded in church books; certificates are handed out. But now Jesus pointed to another baptism, that of the Spirit. Different from water baptism, the baptism of the Spirit is totally invisible. No photos can capture it because the kingdom of God works from the inside and grows like the mustard seed, salt, or yeast. Names of those receiving this baptism are not recorded by the church secretary in books. They can be recorded only in the books of heaven.

It was Jesus' last day on earth. The final message had been given; the Redeemer longed for reassurance that they at last understood the spiritual nature of His kingdom. Then, one of them raised his hand and asked a question: "Lord, will You at this time restore the kingdom to Israel?" (Acts 1:6). How painful!

Imagine the letdown Jesus must have felt. There He was, ready to ascend, and His beloved disciples still hadn't understood the mission. In His final recorded words, He tells them how to build the spiritual kingdom, a glorious church, without spot or wrinkle, the bride He hopes to meet when He returns. "You shall receive power when the Holy Spirit has come upon you; and you shall be witnesses to Me in Jerusalem, and in all Judea and Samaria, and to the end of the earth" (Acts 1:8). To build the kingdom of God, every disciple will have to become a witness. Without the personal testimony of each and every Christian, the kingdom of God would never exist.

More than twenty centuries have passed since that day, and each must ask him- or herself these questions, Do I understand the spiritual nature of the kingdom of God? Am I helping to build His kingdom, or am I simply following a human agenda? Is simply labeling what I am building "kingdom of God" enough to make it that? Could it be that while I think I am building the Lord's kingdom, I am merely promoting a human kingdom, one that I like to call the "kingdom of God"?

In order to answer these questions, it is necessary to understand first the nature of God's kingdom. It is not made out of material things but of human beings; they represent its basic material, if we can refer to lives in those terms. These are people prepared to meet the returning King: men and women who reflect the character of Jesus, beautiful people who, when they walk down the streets, illuminate the world with the glory of the Lord.

Ellen White describes these people:

> The last message of mercy to be given to the world, is a revelation of His character of love. The children of God are to manifest His glory. In their own life and character they are to reveal what the grace of God has done for them (*Christ's Object Lessons,* pp. 415, 416).

The great purpose of the kingdom of God is redeeming people. Despite the fact that it is a spiritual kingdom, much of its work still takes place on this earth, and for that reason it needs a visible structure. That's why while we continue to live in this world; the kingdom of God needs churches, chapels, publishing houses, hospitals, money, and accounting records. The structure is part of the spiritual kingdom of God; it can't be separated from the kingdom as long as we are pilgrims on this planet.

The danger lies in confusing kingdom and structure, in trying to measure the growth of the kingdom of God by focusing on the structure's expansion. Let me ask a pointed question: Is it possible to achieve structural growth without simultaneously achieving growth in the kingdom of God?

I want to share an incident that illustrates my point. During 1988 we were busy preparing to hold the largest evangelistic series in the history of the church in Brazil. Twenty thousand people were expected nightly at the great covered Ibirapuera Stadium in

São Paulo. This ambitious vision depended on the active participation of many wonderful workers—people who cheerfully gave hours of work and sacrificial financial donations. Two businessmen wanted to get involved in a massive publicity campaign, using a variety of communication media. Consequently, we met with a group of professionals from an advertising firm. One of them asked us: "What kind of public are you going after? We can fill the stadium with the kind of people you prefer—youth, women, elderly people, handicapped—whatever you want."

My first reaction was that this man was simply arrogant, but as he continued, I began to see how powerful advertising really can be. The world practically follows what publicity dictates. Rarely do consumers go for anything other than what the commercials push in their faces—cars, clothes, prepared foods, beauty products, and on and on. The presenter proudly affirmed, for example, that Coca-Cola had become something on the order of a new religion because of marketing. "Who do you think made Coca-Cola what it is today in Brazil? I'll tell you, it was us!"

At that moment, one of my colleagues posed a question: "And if we wanted to mount a publicity blitz promoting our church, would that swell the number of new members?"

"Without a doubt," the man replied. "The only thing is you would need about ten years to build churches, halls, stadiums, and all that sort of thing, because, after all, with your present infrastructure, where could you put all the people who would join your church as a result of our professional services?"

Frankly, I was perplexed. That man wasn't exaggerating. Publicity can sell just about anything, including a philosophy of life. So why do we need the Holy Spirit? Leading crowds of people into church membership shouldn't be that hard; raking in more money and putting up more schools, publishing houses, and churches would clearly not be impossible if left to skilled human hands.

If we were to hire a successful CEO like the ones who have accomplished the explosive growth of companies such as Google, Apple, Honda, and Microsoft, wouldn't it be possible to do the same, causing our church to fabulously expand its consumer base? Not much need then for the Holy Spirit; all we need is sharp business know-how. With this kind of executive genius, after about three years, the books would show amazing results, with lines shooting off the graph, illustrating membership numbers, financial growth, and development around the world. Denominational wealth in property holdings would soar. But here's the bottom line: would all that success reflect the glory of God and the character of Jesus Christ?

By applying leadership and administrative techniques alone, it is possible to grow the structure of the church without necessarily adding to the kingdom of God. At the same time, it is impossible to grow God's kingdom without some structural growth.

My motivation in writing this book is to address the danger we face of misunderstanding what really constitutes the kingdom of God. That was the tragedy among Jesus' disciples, and it could turn out to be our great failure as well. Today, the kingdom of God is equipped with institutions, members, statistics, budgets, and accountants; but the kingdom is much more than just that. If we Christians fail to grow spiritually, if the church fails to lead each new convert to a life of continuing communion with God, if Christians cease praying, studying the Bible, and leading others to Jesus' feet, then we aren't participating in the kingdom of God.

It would be disastrous if we come to believe that expanding the kingdom of God is simply a numbers game. If our enthusiasm to swell the kingdom of God focuses on strategies to increase membership and income, we misunderstand the purpose of the kingdom. Just about any great executive could grow the structure. If that is all we want, there's no need for the Holy Spirit. The challenge to the church is to help each member grow spiritually, which, in turn, will increase membership and financial support.

* * * * *

It is evening as I finish writing this chapter at a hotel in Atlanta. To my right is a window out of which I can see cars heading to their destinations. I think about the drivers behind the wheel, and I feel sorrow for their pain—the pain of living without Christ. Then, I hear again Jesus' challenge: "Go invite people to become part of My kingdom. Don't simply make them members of the church; help them become truly spiritual men and women. For this purpose I promise you the gift of My Spirit."

Questions to Consider

1. Why did Jesus teach His disciples by means of parables?
2. Why did the disciples so often fail to understand the Master's teachings?
3. Do we understand the Word of the Lord in our time?
4. How difficult it is to bring a person to Jesus' feet?

Chapter 2
God's Dream

The night is already dark. I feel compelled to sit at the writing desk in my hotel room. I turn on my computer. "Dear Lord," I plead, "wrap me in Your arms, open the portals of heaven, and shine Your thoughts into my mind." My fingers hover lightly over the keyboard; thoughts of human sorrows and suffering overwhelm me.

* * * * *

The world moaned while trapped in the darkness of sin. All the inhabited universe wept, for every man and woman stood condemned to eternal death. But the the Lord Jesus had a dream for their redemption: He would rescue His children from evil, restore in them the image of the Father, and present them as "a glorious church, without spot or wrinkle or any such thing" at His second coming (Ephesians 5:27).

But every dream has a price tag attached. Jesus paid a supremely high price for His dream; it cost Him His life. Paul affirms that "Christ . . . loved the church and gave Himself for her" (verse 25). He gave Himself as a sacrifice and died. "He was led as a lamb to the slaughter, and as a sheep before its shearers is silent, so He opened not His mouth" (Isaiah 53:7).

In the Bible we find God's magnificent dream described again and again. Close your eyes and in your imagination visualize the glory suggested in the following verse:

Who is she who looks forth as the morning,
Fair as the moon,
Clear as the sun,
Awesome as an army with banners?
(Song of Solomon 6:10).

This is God's dream! A people prepared, a glorious church without stain, fair as the moon, clear as the sun, reflecting the character of God. This church is composed of human beings capable of hearing the melodious voice of the Father who says,

Arise, shine;
For your light has come!
And the glory of the LORD is risen upon you.
For behold, the darkness shall cover the earth,
And deep darkness the people;
But the LORD will arise over you,
And His glory will be seen upon you.
The Gentiles shall come to your light,
And kings to the brightness of your rising
(Isaiah 60:1–3).

It's a glorious church, pure and spotless, like a bride dressed in purest white, awaiting her bridegroom. Picture an authentic, genuine church, with nothing artificial or political, "not with eyeservice, as men-pleasers, but as bondservants of Christ, doing the will of God from the heart, with goodwill doing service, as to the Lord, and not to men" (Ephesians 6:6, 7). This is the church that fulfills God's dreams! These are the subjects of the Father's kingdom.

The day is soon approaching, and it will not be delayed, when Jesus will appear in the clouds of heaven, arriving to claim the church of His dreams. On that day, the question He will ask us will not concern numbers—how many people I led into the baptistry, how many new congregations I organized, or how many church buildings I helped erect. Don't get me wrong; all of that has its useful place while God's faithful ones march onward in this present world. But clearly, the question He wants answered has little to do with statistics. It has everything to do with the dream that led Him to the Cross. *Where is the glorious church that I asked you to help prepare for our encounter?*

I fear that on that day, the apologies I mumble will fall pitifully short of justifying my failure to meet His expectation; what lame excuses could I offer to Jesus? Sorry, I was so busy conducting evangelistic campaigns that I just couldn't squeeze in time for preparing the glorious church! Sorry, I had a baptism goal, and that left me no time to help prepare Your church.

The Lord Jesus asked me to help prepare a glorious church, one that reflects the glory of God. This is His greatest desire; it is also the mission with which He has entrusted me. How can I carry out this divine dream? How can I help the church in reflecting the glory of God?

First of all, I need to understand what is meant by "the glory of God." What is the glory of God? Ellen White helps us answer this very question:

> "Pray with Moses, 'Show me Thy glory.' What is this glory?—the character of God" (*Testimonies to Ministers,* p. 499).

God expects His church to reflect His character. But sin has disfigured His reflection in our lives. Jesus came to this world in order to reproduce in human beings the character of the Father. He left all behind in heaven and came to this world of misery and pain to pay the price of our restoration. For this reason,

Christ is waiting with longing desire for the manifestation of Himself in His church. When the character of Christ shall be perfectly reproduced in His people, then He will come to claim them as His own (*Christ's Object Lessons,* p. 69).

The Lord Jesus patiently waits for the church to reflect His character before He will come to receive His people.

Let's review a similar statement that was introduced in the previous chapter:

The last rays of merciful light, the last message of mercy to be given to the world, is a revelation of His character of love. The children of God are to manifest His glory. In their own life and character they are to reveal what the grace of God has done for them (*Christ's Object Lessons,* pp. 415, 416).

What an amazing challenge! The last message to be given to the world is not theoretical. It is not merely the teaching of a body of doctrinal beliefs. Instead, it has everything to do with manifesting God's glory.

We are to go forth to proclaim the goodness of God and to make plain His real character before the people. We are to reflect His glory. Have we done this in the past? Have we revealed the character of our Lord by precept and example? (*Faith and Works,* p. 61).

To what degree have I understood this? Just how seriously am I concerned about building the church of God's dreams? What does it mean to prepare a church that reflects the character of Jesus?

How does one go about building His kingdom?

When we study chapter 6 of the letter to the Ephesians, we find the tools that God provides for building such a church. The apostle Paul presents them metaphorically as pieces of armor:

> Therefore take up the whole armor of God, that you may be able to withstand in the evil day, and having done all, to stand. Stand therefore, having girded your waist with *truth,* having put on the breastplate of *righteousness,* and having shod your feet with *the preparation of the gospel of peace;* above all, taking the shield of *faith* with which you will be able to quench all the fiery darts of the wicked one. And take the helmet of *salvation,* and the sword of the Spirit, which is *the word of God;* praying always with all **prayer** and supplication in the Spirit, being watchful to this end with all perseverance and supplication for all the saints (Ephesians 6:13–18; emphasis added).

The church that clads itself with the godly armor will "be able to withstand in the evil day, and having done all, to stand," firmly reflecting the glory of God. Now *that* will be a well-approved church, just as the apostle declares! Remember, then, the necessary tools to reflect the glory of God are truth, righteousness, preparation of the gospel of peace, faith, salvation, the Word of God, and prayer.

We need to examine the armor more closely. Let's divide the armor into two groups. In the first group, we will place truth, righteousness, faith, and salvation. God places these four divine instruments in human hands, but man's participation is limited to accepting or rejecting them.

The second group of three includes prayer, daily Bible study, and preparation of the gospel of peace. These are also divine gifts, but they apply only if a person puts them into practice. The Christian's participation in using these three pieces of armor is much more active. Let me explain it a little further: you and I can neither add to nor subtract from truth, righteousness, faith, or salvation; all we can do is either accept them or reject them. They are always available, quite independent of human control. But in the case of gospel preparation, daily Bible study, and prayer, our participation is indispensable. We are the ones who have to daily pray and study the Bible. God is not going to take our place and do that for us.

We all know what prayer and Bible study mean, but what does "preparation of the gospel of peace" mean? Isaiah explains it for us:

> How beautiful upon the mountains
> Are the feet of him who brings good news,
> Who proclaims peace,
> Who brings glad tidings of good things,
> Who proclaims salvation,
> Who says to Zion,
> "Your God reigns!"
> (Isaiah 52:7).

Preparation of the gospel of peace amounts to bringing people to Christ. We can call it witnessing. It is an indispensable component in the process of personal spiritual growth. And spiritual growth has as its fundamental objective preparing us to reflect the character of Jesus Christ.

Many Christians manage to pray and study their Bibles day after day. The difficulty for most is leading people to Jesus' feet. Sincere believers, well intentioned as they undoubtedly are, try and try again, but all too frequently end up frustrated when they attempt to lead others to Jesus. After a few failures, they come to the conclusion that they simply have no gift for witnessing. However, from the divine point of view, to pray, to study the Bible, and to lead people to Jesus are not gifts. They are key tools for Christian growth. The use of these tools determines our growth in God's grace.

In order for these tools to achieve God's intended results, they need to work together. We could illustrate the concept by comparing it to the use of dynamite. Dynamite has three elements: powder, a detonator, and a fuse. If any of the three are missing, there will be no blast. On the other hand, if the three elements are correctly combined, the scene is set for a spectacular wallop. The same thing happens in your spiritual life. Prayer and Bible study without witnessing make for an incomplete formula. Such a combination, without the third element, may well lead to fanaticism or mysticism. Ellen White warns that

> we are in the waiting time. But this period is not to be spent in abstract devotion. Waiting, watching, and vigilant working are to be combined (*Christian Service,* p. 85).

Exactly what does the servant of the Lord mean by "abstract devotion"? To me, she clearly means prayer and Bible study by themselves, without the work of leading others to Jesus' feet. One thing is for sure, if you make witnessing an active part of your devotional life, you will soon experience a new and extraordinary level of growth toward reflecting God's glory.

> It is as we give ourselves to God for the service of humanity that He gives Himself to us (*Thoughts From the Mount of Blessing,* p. 81).

Bert was a respected church elder, always faithful to his duties; he was a dedicated father and an extraordinary husband. Everyone loved him at church; the members looked up to him and wanted to be like him. Nobody knew, however, of the deep emptiness Bert felt in his heart. He would pass entire nights tossing and turning without a clue to the cause of his sleeplessness. He lived an exemplary moral life just as all Christians should. On the surface, there was no obvious reason for his anxiety; still, he was deeply unhappy. That's when he decided to write me a letter. He wrote about the good things he always tried to do for God. Then he asked if that was all there was to the Christian life, or if he was somehow missing something.

As I read Bert's letter, I soon began to see that he was talking about everything except the persons he had led to Jesus' feet. Suddenly it became clear to me why Bert was unsure about his Christian experience. He was faithful about praying and reading the Bible daily, but in recent months, he had lost the zest for personal devotions. Naturally, that worried him. He felt like a phony, knowing how others looked up to him. Sabbath School lesson study had become a Friday night marathon; after all, he had to teach the class the following morning.

I decided to respond to Bert's letter, spelling out the believer's need to look for someone to lead to Jesus. Bert did not reply to my letter, and I assumed he hadn't followed up on my suggestion. But sometime later, while attending a church convention, he looked me up, and reminded me about his letter and my reply. Then, full of emotion, Bert expressed these sentiments: "Pastor, your letter came filled with words of wisdom. Today I am a different person, full of real happiness. I have brought two persons to Christ this past year; now once again I feel that first love which I had lost."

This is such a simple truth to learn and yet, for some reason, the most difficult to put into practice. Nobody can grow in personal Christianity—it is impossible to enjoy the thrill of the victorious life—without including in one's devotional life the experience of bringing another person to Jesus.

Could it be that right now you are feeling frustrated because so many times you tried but failed to do this? Allow me to tell you that there is no need to fear. Witnessing can be fascinating. It doesn't have to be complicated; it is easier than you imagine. To begin with, let me put your mind at ease regarding a few specific fears—you don't have to give Bible studies, knock on the doors of total strangers, or lead out in evangelistic meetings.

Great! But then you wonder, *Just how am I going to bring people to Jesus?* Friend, that is what this book is going to attempt to accomplish: teaching you to share Jesus. The day you learn the *how to* will put you on the road to winning souls within a year. Soul winning will make you sense the need of continuing prayer and Bible study every day, and as you do that, you will find yourself participating in God's dream. Your spiritual experience will blossom, and you will become a living part of the glorious church, without spot or wrinkle, that Jesus is coming to receive. Wouldn't you love to live such an experience?

Questions to Consider

1. What is God's dream for us?
2. How is His kingdom built?
3. To what degree am I concerned with building the church of God's dreams?
4. What does it mean to prepare a church that reflects the character of Jesus?
5. How can I inspire other church members to become enthusiastic about building the church of God's dreams?

Chapter 3

The Reason Behind the Mission

It's Sunday night. Anguish and fear hang heavy over the group. The disciples face one of their darkest and most discouraging nights ever. The Master is no longer with them; two days earlier, He was brutally nailed to a cross and left to die like a common criminal. He didn't demand justice—He didn't so much as protest the abuse. How could He have let His kingdom go undefended like that? Now, He's dead and in the tomb, leaving His followers all alone. Yet, they can't get Him out of their minds. Then something stirs the curtains though the window shutters are closed. Faces pale; hearts pound.

The apostle John describes the incident: "Then, the same day at evening, being the first day of the week, when the doors were shut where the disciples were assembled, for fear of the Jews, Jesus came and stood in the midst, and said to them, 'Peace be with you' " (John 20:19).

When you think of it, how comforting it is to realize that Jesus always draws near in the darkest nights of our lives. Just when we haven't a clue about where to go or what to do, at the moment when we've nearly reached the end of our rope, there He stands, ready to restore peace to our trembling hearts.

Jesus appeared to His disciples that dreary Sunday night for the purpose of resolving a serious problem that, if not addressed, would soon destroy them. They were dejected and anxious. Fear can paralyze you. It robs you of joy, it wrings you dry and saps your will to live. A fearful person is incapable of winning, finding fulfillment, or growing. Jesus realized that these men needed strengthening. Then, mysteriously, He was among them, and with these words He soothed their anxiety: "Peace to you! As the Father has sent Me, I also send you" (John 20:21).

What a weird way to counter fear! According to John, the Master assigned the disciples a mission to free them from fear's grip. If they could be kept busy with His work assignment, there would be no time for them to focus on their fears. As their courage developed, victories would follow. He knew that soon these men could become unstoppable witnesses of His love.

There are many Christians today who, despite knowing Jesus, are dominated by fear. They fear persecution, they fear their past, the future, death, not being saved, not doing God's will, and so much more. The glorious church awaiting Christ's return should not be defined by fear and trembling. The cure Jesus prescribes for His people is to become fully involved in fulfilling the Great Commission. Those who are dedicated to sharing Jesus don't have time to be driven by fear or anxiety.

Let's take a look at what Matthew says concerning the purpose behind the Great Commission. "The eleven disciples went away into Galilee, to the mountain which Jesus had appointed for them. When they saw Him, they worshiped Him; but some doubted. And Jesus came and spoke to them, saying, 'All authority has been given to Me in heaven and on earth. Go therefore and make disciples of all the nations' " (Matthew 28:16–19).

According to Matthew, the shadow enshrouding the disciples at the time of Jesus' resurrection was doubt. "Some doubted," the Scripture bluntly states. A life filled with doubt can't be happy. A Christianity weakened with doubts isn't healthy. The church of God's dream has learned the virtues of trust and assurance. A life filled with doubt is on the path to self-destruction. Christianity should lead us to experience trust and certainty. At least, these should be much more prominent than doubt.

What did Jesus do to help His disciples overcome doubt? He didn't explain much; He simply gave them the mission. He rallied them: "Go therefore and make disciples of all the nations." In Jesus' mind, the best medicine for doubt, and even heresy or dissidence, is a hearty commitment to the mission. The life of a person who is committed to leading others to Christ has little room for doubt.

Mark records the commission in his Gospel as well. "Later He appeared to the eleven as they sat at the table; and He rebuked their unbelief and hardness of heart, because they did not believe those who had seen Him after He had risen. And He said to them, 'Go into all the world and preach the gospel to every creature' " (Mark 16:14, 15).

In Mark's opinion, the main problem affecting the disciples was that of "unbelief and hardness of heart." They had a hard time believing. Their hearts were cold and unfeeling. What is the cure for this problem, according to Mark's Gospel? Once again we see that it comes down to Jesus' simply entrusting them with the mission. Nothing works better for a person plagued by unbelief than becoming personally involved in mission.

When I was a young pastor, a church member came up to me one day and said skeptically, "Pastor, I think you must be making up those conversion stories you like to tell in your sermons. I've never met anyone with such dramatic stories."

"And how many people have you brought to Jesus?" I asked him in response.

The man looked down in embarrassment, but became interested when I invited him to accompany me that afternoon to a prison where I was conducting meetings among people who were doing time for crimes they had committed. He soon became so enthusiastic about participating, that within a few months he was ready to take charge of the prison meetings. Every time he came by to tell me fresh and extraordinary stories from his prison ministry, I would smile at him and would playfully banter, "Look here, Brother, are you sure of those facts? Sounds to me like just another whopper!"

He would laugh. His problem was resolved. He doubted no more. In the life of a person who is wholeheartedly committed to the mission, there's no place for unbelief and hardness of heart.

Finally, I want us to look into what Luke has to say concerning the reason behind the Great Commission. "They were terrified and frightened, and supposed they had seen a spirit. And He said to them, 'Why are you troubled? And why do doubts arise in your hearts?' . . .

"Then He said to them, 'Thus it is written, and thus it was necessary for the Christ to suffer and to rise from the dead the third day, and that repentance and remission of sins should be preached in His name to all nations' " (Luke 24:37, 38, 46, 47).

According to Luke's story, the problem with the disciples on that occasion was terror and fear. The circumstances were frightening, and the disciples seemed to have little reserves of trust in the divine promises. They were overwhelmed with apprehension. And again, Jesus, in order to help them overcome their fear, entrusted them with the mission.

After taking part in a seminar on evangelism during which I spoke about the importance of every Christian being actively involved, a like-minded colleague in the ministry shared with me the following story. A church member would constantly call for the pastor's help. She was under the impression that her strange neighbor was using dark arts to seduce her husband. The woman lived in constant worry about what new spell her neighbor might be casting. But this wasn't her only fear. Every little event rattled her; her nerves were always on edge. Whenever a thunderstorm rolled through, this sister would grab the phone, call the pastor, and tearfully beg for his prayers even if "only over the wires."

My colleague said to me, "I couldn't keep facilitating that church sister's dependence on me, so one day I finally made a deal with her. 'My dear sister, I will continue praying for you as many times as you want, at any time of the day or night, but only on one condition. I am going to give you the name and address of someone I want you to visit. You can give her Bible studies.' The church member accepted my offer. It wasn't very long until her worried calls ended."

This sister became so enthusiastic with the mission of leading another person to Jesus' feet, that her life no longer contained room for fear. Her problem was solved.

Ah, yes, my friends, when the Lord Jesus entrusted believers with the mission of bringing people to His kingdom, it wasn't because He couldn't evangelize the world all by Himself. After all, God is God! For Him nothing is impossible. Notice what Ellen White says,

> God could have reached His object in saving sinners without our aid (*The Desire of Ages,* p. 142).

Yes, He certainly could have. So why doesn't He just evangelize the world Himself? It isn't that He doesn't want to or that He can't. Sometimes we hear folks say that we must preach the gospel in order to finish the work—if we don't, Jesus won't return. That simply is not true. When in God's calendar the day and the hour arrive for Christ to appear in the clouds, you can be absolutely sure that the Father will send Him on His way. The Second Coming does not depend on our work. To preach the gospel to the whole world in an instant poses no problem to God. He could do the job

Himself, or through the ministry of angels. Ellen White tells us that

> God could have proclaimed His truth through sinless
> angels, but this is not His plan (*The Acts of the Apostles*,
> p. 330).

Of course the angels would willingly complete the mission, but the fact is that angels do not *need* the benefits that come from such ministry. We human beings are the ones who *need* the blessings that come from participating. You can clearly see this fact revealed in the following statement:

> The angel sent to Philip could himself have done the work
> for the Ethiopian, but this is not God's way of working
> (*The Acts of the Apostles*, p. 109).

If the angel had the message in his hands, why did he waste time looking for Philip? The angel could have located the Ethiopian and given him the Bible study. But that is not the way it worked, because the angel had no personal need for growth in his spiritual experience. The mission was entrusted to humans so that they could grow in their relationship with Christ. God has other means by which the gospel can be preached. But if we want to form part of the church that reflects the glory of God and is prepared to meet Jesus in His majesty, then we need to participate in the mission:

> It is as we give ourselves to God for the service of human-
> ity that He gives Himself to us (*Thoughts From the Mount
> of Blessing*, p. 81).

The mission is the divine instrument that makes it possible for

Christians to grow. This is not an assignment to be carried out by only a small group of volunteers. The mission is for each individual, one by one, because each child of God needs to grow.

> Those who stand as leaders in the church of God are to realize that the Saviour's commission is given to all who believe in His name (*The Acts of the Apostles,* p. 110).

What a dramatic declaration! We leaders are called to understand that church growth is not about contracting Bible workers and professional evangelists so that these professionals can bring in great numbers of baptismal candidates to swell church membership rolls. Evangelistic campaigns, efforts by Bible workers, and baptism of new believers are all good and right. How marvelous when those ministries are fed by individual efforts made by each Christian. If such activities merely promote statistical growth while leaving church members with arms folded, observing from the sidelines, then the church has failed. It is one of the worst things that can happen in the life of the church.

The following chapter will demonstrate a simple way for Christian believers to lead people to Christ.

Questions to Consider

1. What is the underlying purpose of the Great Commission?
2. Are prayer, Bible study, and the commission all on the same level?
3. Is the pastor ultimately responsible for carrying out the commission?
4. How do I feel when I am left standing on the sidelines while soul winning takes place?
5. If I don't know how to conduct Bible studies, how else can I participate in the Great Commission?

Chapter 4

The Gospel Became Flesh

"Pastor, please help me. I've been a member of the church for the past twenty years, but I've never yet led a single soul to Christ. I'm afraid I'm going to be lost!" This brother's plea reveals the silent concern of many Christians who want to participate in the Great Commission, and yet are afraid to do so. The purpose of this chapter is to demonstrate that sharing Jesus comes naturally in the life of one who has met the Lord.

The first thing to understand about leading people to Christ is that it needs to be carried out in harmony with the divine concept of evangelism. What did God do to make salvation available to human beings? How did He go about reaching them with the gospel message? What were the initial steps He put into practice in the process of spreading the gospel? Let's look back at these questions. The apostle John says, "In the beginning was the Word, and the Word was with God, and the Word was God" (John 1:1).

God the Father was in heaven together with His Son. The Lord Jesus Christ, besides being the Son, was also the Word, the Message, the Gospel, and the very Fountain of salvation. None of these could possibly exist without Jesus. In the Father's great heart, there was a deep desire to offer the gospel of salvation to the world; He yearned to save His children and to share with them the good news of redemption. This is evangelism. So, how did He accomplish it? The key is in John 1:14: "The Word became flesh and dwelt among us, and we beheld His glory, the glory as of the only begotten of the Father, full of grace and truth."

In this verse we see where the process of evangelism began. The Word became flesh; in other words, He put on humanity. And, having taken human form and being born into the world as a baby boy, He grew up and lived among fellow human beings, His manner of relating to them "full of grace and truth." From early on in His human existence, Jesus saw the pain, the struggle, and the difficulties they had to face. He pondered the effects of sin and was filled with compassion for people, even to the point of giving up His own life out of love for them.

While Jesus was busy fulfilling His ministry and traveling around Palestine, something more was taking place. Thousands were turning their attention to Him and beginning to perceive the glory of God. The expression "the glory of God" is key to understanding evangelism from the divine perspective. The world of Jesus' time was evangelized because the Gospel became flesh and lived among humans, reflecting the glory of the Father. To evangelize, according to John, is to allow the gospel to transcend theory and be revealed in the flesh, through the person's life and relationships. For you and for me it is much easier to believe in what we see rather than what we are told. Similarly, if people are really going to believe in Jesus, they will need to see the glory of God.

To evangelize is to show God's glory to human beings. This glory is the character of God. That is how God, in the person of the Son, evangelized the world. "He who has seen Me has seen the Father" (John 14:9), insisted Jesus. He was the Incarnation of the gospel; He was the Light that shines in this dark world. "In Him was life, and the life was the light of men" (John 1:4).

During His time interacting with men and women, Jesus stated, "As long as I am in the world, I am the light of the world" (John 9:5). Then, just before being lifted up on Calvary's cross, He declared, "A little while longer the light is with you" (John 12:35). Why did Jesus claim to be the Light of the world? Because in Him the gospel came alive in a human person, and in His life, He reflected the glory of God.

But then Jesus died, was resurrected, and returned to heaven and to the Father. He left this message for each of us: "You are the light of the world" (Matthew 5:14). The apostle Paul emphasized that point: "now you are light in the Lord. Walk as children of light" (Ephesians 5:8). Paul is categorical when he declares, "You are . . . children of light." Of what light is he speaking? That of Jesus—He who said, "I am the light of the world." And if we are children of the Light, that means we also are transformed into light, and we reflect the glory of the Father just as Jesus our Lord did. For this very reason, in chapter 5 of the letter to the Ephesians, Paul describes the church of God's dreams as "glorious . . . not having spot or wrinkle or any such thing" (verse 27). The focus once again is on the expression *glorious*. Those Christians in whose lives the gospel has become incarnated are part of the glorious church because they reflect the character of Jesus.

Let's move on to the concept of light. While Jesus was still on earth, He was the Light of the world. That is also our role. What is the purpose of light? It is to illuminate. And how does it accomplish its purpose? It doesn't hold a shine-a-thon campaign; it simply does what God ordained it to do. All that is needed to dispel the shadows is a good source of light; usually flipping on the light switch brightens every corner. When there is light, darkness vanishes. We are the light of this world. Evangelism means illuminating this sinful world with the light of the gospel. All we need to share the gospel is that it becomes a reality in our lives, turning us into sources of light. That's what Jesus was getting at when He said, "You are the light of the world. A city that is set on a hill cannot be hidden" (Matthew 5:14).

It's impossible for light not to illuminate. If every Christian is a lighted lantern, if the gospel becomes flesh in our lives, if all of us come to reflect the glory of God, it will be virtually impossible for the world to remain unaffected. I'll say it again; the first thing that is needed is to internalize the gospel deep into our inner being. If we nod our heads in agreement with that, but plod on using the same old strategies and tactics aimed merely at swelling membership numbers, then we haven't learned a thing—and we will surely fail.

The Lord Jesus repeated this concept of evangelism using many different similes. On one occasion, He said, "You are the salt of the earth" (Matthew 5:13). How is salt useful? It adds flavor to food. And how does that happen? Salt doesn't hold evangelistic meetings. It simply mingles with the ingredients and enhances the flavor. We are the salt of the earth. We need to add the perfect seasoning to the world's melting pot of humanity. By reflecting the glory of God, we can exercise positive transformations even in the structures of society. Just as yeast permeates the dough (see Matthew 13:33), we are to exhibit godliness in our surrounding communities. Just as the soil accepts the seed (see Matthew 13:31), we are to sprout and bless the field with a bumper crop of righteousness. We are God's quality seed.

You most likely have noticed that not one of these elements used to symbolize God's church achieves the goal by means of impressive campaigns. As long as individual members fail to fulfill their roles as light, salt, yeast, or seed, the religious organization will wander aimlessly along, inventing "methods" that end up as worthless substitutes for the kind of gospel work Christ assigned to His followers. We leaders have the responsibility to keep clearly in mind the true plan of God for His church.

It is the divine plan that His people—those in whose lives the gospel has been made flesh—shall circulate in the world, full of "grace and truth." And what does this biblical term mean? The Greek word for *truth* is *aleteia*, which literally means "open window," or "that which is not shut," "transparent." In order to live the truth transparently, Christians need to reflect the character of Jesus. The servant of the Lord says,

> God could have reached His object in saving sinners with-
> out our aid; but in order for us to develop a character like
> Christ's, we must share in His work. In order to enter into
> His joy—the joy of seeing souls redeemed by His sacrifice—
> we must participate in His labors for their redemption
> (*The Desire of Ages,* p. 142).

King David describes such people clearly.

> Lord, who may abide in Your tabernacle?
> Who may dwell in Your holy hill?
> He who walks uprightly,
>   And works righteousness,
>   And speaks the truth in his heart
>   (Psalm 15:1, 2).

Here, the word *truth,* in its Hebrew original, is *emeth,* which means
"sure," "solid," "firm," or "consistent." In order for Christians to per-
severe in truth with firmness, strength, and consistency,

> well-organized work must be done in the church, that its
> members may understand how to impart the light to oth-
> ers and thus strengthen their own faith and increase their
> knowledge. As they impart that which they have received
> from God they will be confirmed in the faith. A working
> church is a living church (*Testimonies,* vol. 6, p. 435).

Having read this far in the book, you probably have noted that
this work of leading people to Jesus' feet is both cause and effect. You
witness because you reflect the glory of God, but you also reflect the

glory of God because you are out there witnessing. The two aspects are inseparable and are mutually supportive. You mature in Christian experience because you witness, and you just naturally witness because the character of Jesus is shining out through your life.

Difficulties arise when the linkage is broken between those two interlocking features. Many seem to hope for spiritual growth in their lives, but they want growth without having to share Jesus. Others want to mass-market Jesus to the waiting world by means of human marketing techniques, forgetting that in the divine pattern, real witnessing flows only from personally reflecting God's glory and His character. Sharing Christ from within our individual lives is what powers heaven-ordained evangelism.

The light that attracts others and helps them decide for Christ is the undeniable revelation of Jesus' character shining from balanced, mature Christians. When these people are in public, Jesus can be seen in them. When they chat with neighbors, friends, and loved ones who still haven't embraced the gospel, it is Jesus who is shining through them. "He who has seen Me has seen the Father," Jesus said (John 14:9). And he who has seen this kind of Christian will perceive Jesus. "It is no longer I who live, but Christ lives in me," as Paul puts it (Galatians 2:20).

This concept is depicted in two of Jesus' parables recorded in the Gospel of Matthew. In the parable of the sower, the seed represents the Word of God (Matthew 13:19). But in the next parable that the Master relates—the one about the tares—the seed no longer represents the Word; instead, it now symbolizes the children of God's kingdom who receive the Word (verse 38). The Word now becomes flesh in the sons of the kingdom, and now these become the seed.

Ellen White explains Jesus' method of evangelism when He was on earth:

Often the inhabitants of a city where Christ labored wished Him to stay with them and continue to work among them. But He would tell them that He must go to cities that had not heard the truths that He had to present. After He had given the truth to those in one place, He left them to build upon what He had given them, while He went to another place. His methods of labor are to be followed today by those to whom He has left His work (*Counsels on Health,* p. 396).

Jesus sowed the seed in the hearts of His listeners and then looked for them to become gospel seed. In that way, the multiplication factor set in. You don't need to become nervous over the idea of having to win people to Christ. It's not as difficult as you might imagine. What you need to do is simply be yourself in the transformed life Jesus clothes you with. Carry on with all your daily activities, but with the enriched purpose of sharing the same good news with others that brought peace to your own heart. You don't have to separate blocks of additional time from your already loaded agenda in order to do "missionary work." Essentially, you simply shine with the light of Jesus while interacting with your friends and relatives, neighbors and colleagues. You are simply being yourself. That's all.

"But, Pastor," you ask, "do you think that following such a plan is going to draw people to Jesus? When am I supposed to give them Bible studies?"

Don't get ahead of yourself. Everything has its time and place, as the wise man said. For now, just start living your wonderful experience with the loving Savior, nothing more. Let the story flow naturally and gently along.

Throughout my ministry, I have seen the Holy Spirit work on many hearts. I remember a drunken man who came one night to a church meeting. For many years, he had been a slave to addiction; he beat his wife, mistreated his children, and wasted all his wages on alcohol. But that particular night as he was stumbling down the street, he noticed that the church door was open and the lights were on. He was ready to collapse and what better spot than on a church bench! Somehow, right through the drunken fog, the Spirit of God was able to interject words from my sermon into his mind. To everyone's astonishment, when I made the altar call for people to come forward, here came the drunkard, holding on to the benches as he walked up the aisle, but joining the others. The deacon thought this man's decision worthless. "But, Pastor, surely we don't need to fill out a decision card for this man. He is so drunk that he doesn't know where he is or what is going on." Despite appearances, the Spirit of God had truly touched that man, and even though he didn't fully realize what was going on around him, he believed that Jesus could work a miracle for him.

The next evening the same man returned to the meeting; this time he was not drunk. The following night and then the night after that—he kept showing up. When the series of meetings came to its end, that former drunk had gone through the Bible lessons lucidly and had given his heart to Jesus. His life was totally changed! In the place of a heart of stone, Jesus had given him a heart of flesh. Then he searched for his wife and family. He begged their forgiveness for all the misery he had caused them. When they finally could see that he was genuinely changed, they, of course, wanted to know how such a thing had happened.

"What in the world has happened that you are now so different?" they asked him.

"Come with me and see for yourselves what has happened," he replied.

So, one night soon after that, he brought his wife and children to church. They began to attend regularly, and when there was another altar call, the entire family came forward. At the end of the meetings, they were all baptized. Today, they are a very happy family. One of the sons eventually went to an Adventist college to prepare for the ministry.

This drunk, with a life wrecked by sin, was transformed when through his stupor he cried out to the Savior. The Spirit prayed with him that night, and God bent down to listen, "Lord, take my heart, give me a new and better one of flesh."

Now this Christian, in whose life the gospel became flesh, has gone on to live the rest of his life with abiding love for the Lord Jesus Christ, witnessing to others about what Jesus has done for him. When Jesus enters your heart, telling others what He did for you becomes your greatest joy. You receive the seed, which is the Word, and then you become seed, ready to announce the good news of salvation to others.

Questions to Consider

1. How did God evangelize the world? Think about how God became flesh in order to evangelize the world.
2. How did Jesus go about evangelizing in His time?
3. What does evangelism mean in your life?
4. What relationship exists between evangelism and the glory of God?
5. What relationship is there between the glory of God and the idea of preparing a people for the coming of Jesus?

Chapter 5

How Did Jesus Want to Evangelize the World?

It's a fine sunny morning in the region of Galilee. John the Baptist and two of his disciples hike along dusty footpaths in the hilly terrain. Suddenly, John spies Jesus, stops in his tracks, and points Him out to his companions. The Gospels tell what happened. "Looking at Jesus as He walked, he said, 'Behold the Lamb of God!' " (John 1:35, 36).

John uplifts Jesus. And what follows? Verse 37 tells us: "The two disciples heard him speak, and they followed Jesus."

That straightforward act sets the stage for what we can expect to see whenever Jesus is uplifted. Jesus Himself said the same thing: "And I, if I am lifted up from the earth, will draw all peoples to Myself" (John 12:32).

When Jesus is lifted up before humanity, few can resist. Something about the Master of Galilee amazingly attracts and then melts hearts; His true Presence generally precludes arguments and objections. Before Jesus, men and women have little choice but to fall at His feet and accept Him as their Savior. That is what happened to those two disciples of John: they followed Jesus and remained with Him. They were, at that moment, born into the kingdom of God.

Let's take a look at what Ellen White says concerning those who are born into the kingdom of God.

Every true disciple is born into the kingdom of God as a missionary. He who drinks of the living water becomes a fountain of life. The receiver becomes a giver (*The Desire of Ages,* p. 195).

A missionary is one who fulfills the mission of pointing others to Jesus. Once you discover the great love of your life, you can no longer remain silent; you need to share your discovery with others.

To fulfill the mission does not mean to proselytize; it is not about stealing sheep from one denomination in order to herd them into a different one. By no means is it a question of making people change religious affiliations. It's about changing lives. To be in the church is a natural consequence of having made a life change. People who hadn't a clue about the meaning of life, who cried themselves to sleep, restless and empty, now come into contact with Jesus, and their lives are so changed that they just can't keep quiet. They have to get out there and tell practically everyone they meet what happened to them. This is a compulsion born of love, a motivation that springs from a totally new perspective on life.

That is what happened to John's disciples. The Bible tells us how Andrew responded, "One of the two who heard John speak, and followed Him, was Andrew, Simon Peter's brother. He first found his own brother Simon, and said to him, 'We have found the Messiah' (which is translated, the Christ)" (John 1:40, 41).

Andrew first found Peter. The key verb here is *to find.* Generally, to find something, you need to search for it. (Be alert, however. The Holy Spirit just may lead you to a person you hadn't thought to look for.) Andrew deliberately went looking for Peter. The excitement of discovering the Messiah was so great that he couldn't keep it to himself, so Andrew hurried to find someone else to bring to Jesus. He hardly needed to give a second thought about whom to tell first—his own brother, Peter. They were very close, as well as being partners in the family fishing business.

It's much more natural to believe someone you know than a

stranger. We learn to mistrust those we don't know. We all know stories of fraud, violence, and misplaced confidence. This makes calling on doors particularly challenging. Very few people are willing to hear what a stranger may have to say. That's why it is almost always difficult to do outreach among those we don't know. Some still push on, trying to literally get feet in the doors of strangers. Then, when the doors are slammed in their faces, they figure it's too difficult to labor there and they look for other tactics to win over people they don't know.

The gospel tells how God wanted to evangelize the world. If we had just followed the biblical model, the world would have been reached by now. Every tribe, language, and people could have long ago heard the plan of salvation, and Jesus would have returned. We would not still be wayfarers in this world of suffering and death.

> Had the purpose of God been carried out by His people in giving to the world the message of mercy, Christ would, ere this, have come to the earth, and the saints would have received their welcome into the city of God (*Testimonies,* vol. 6, p. 449).

What was Andrew's first step in his work of evangelism? He didn't go looking for a total stranger. He didn't knock on the doors of strangers. He looked for his brother, with whom he worked day in and day out, and said to him: "We have found the Messiah." What was the result of speaking about Jesus to someone he already knew? Right away, Peter left with Andrew to see the Lord.

The Christian's mission is to share Jesus. It is the saving Lord who touches hearts and brings about their conversion. Nevertheless, there has to be an Andrew conscious of his mission who knows a Peter to contact and take to see Jesus. Note how Ellen

White explains Heaven's plan for evangelism:

> In His wisdom the Lord brings those who are seeking for truth into touch with fellow beings who know the truth. It is the plan of Heaven that those who have received light shall impart it to those in darkness. Humanity, drawing its efficiency from the great Source of wisdom, is made the instrumentality, the working agency, through which the gospel exercises its transforming power on mind and heart (*The Acts of the Apostles,* p. 134).

The Bible text continues the story of what happened when Andrew took Peter to Jesus. "He brought him to Jesus. Now when Jesus looked at him, He said, 'You are Simon the son of Jonah. You shall be called Cephas' (which is translated, A Stone)" (John 1:42).

In this verse, the Lord describes Peter's past, present, and future. I know your roots, Jesus says to him: "You are the son of Jonah." But He also knows the present: "You are Simon." But most important is the transformation Simon will undergo by Christ's grace: " 'You shall be called Cephas' (which is translated, A Stone)."

This encounter with Jesus changed Peter's life. Andrew's brother left the meeting with a new vision of life. Thrilled and energized, Peter could not avoid telling others what had just happened to him. So what did he do next? Did he run right out the door, looking for a total stranger to confront with his amazing story? Of course not. People almost never want to be bothered by strangers confronting them about matters that don't interest them. Everyone has his own life circumstances to cope with. For that reason, Peter did not go looking for a stranger. The text doesn't come right out and say with whom Peter shared, but from the context, we get the picture in these next verses: "The following day Jesus wanted to go to Galilee, and He found Philip and said to him, 'Follow

Me.' Now Philip was from Bethsaida, the city of Andrew and Peter" (verses 43, 44).

That last sentence gives a major clue. "Philip was from Bethsaida, the city of Andrew and Peter." Why do you suppose that information was included? What do you think John is trying to reveal in that sentence about Peter's eagerness to share his good news?

Bethsaida was just a small place. Nearby lay Capernaum, another small town where everybody knew everyone else. Peter and Philip were neighbors. So, what do people (such as Peter) do when they accept Jesus as their Savior?

> One of the most effective ways in which light can be communicated is by private, personal effort. In the home circle, at your neighbor's fireside, at the bedside of the sick, in a quiet way you may read the Scriptures and speak a word for Jesus and the truth. Thus you may sow precious seed that will spring up and bring forth fruit (*Testimonies,* vol. 6, pp. 428, 429).

Peter looked for his neighbor, Philip, and told him his great discovery. The result was that Philip became a believer, and he responded as every other convert. Here's how Ellen White puts it:

> The very first impulse of the renewed heart is to bring others also to the Saviour (*The Great Controversy,* p. 70).

Next, it is Philip's turn to run with the news, looking for a close friend with whom he can share. "Philip found Nathanael and said to him, 'We have found Him of whom Moses in the law, and also the prophets, wrote—Jesus of Nazareth, the son of Joseph' " (verse 45).

Ellen White describes the encounter between the two friends:

> Philip knew that his friend was searching the prophecies, and while Nathanael was praying under a fig tree, Philip discovered his retreat. They had often prayed together in this secluded spot hidden by the foliage (*The Desire of Ages,* p. 140).

In this quotation, did you notice that word *friend* as well as the statement "they had often prayed together"? Such a relationship is crucial if we want to experience success in fulfilling the gospel commission: friends telling one another what Jesus has done in their lives.

That's how the gospel began to spread; soon the Christian church grew. In the same way, if we are going to obey the Great Commission, we must teach every church member to look for a relative, some close friend, perhaps a work buddy, and then acquaint them with Jesus. Ellen White discusses this method of discipleship:

> In these first few disciples the foundation of the Christian church was being laid by individual effort. John first directed two of his disciples to Christ. Then one of these finds a brother, and brings him to Christ. He then calls Philip to follow him, and he went in search of Nathanael. Here is an instructive lesson for all the followers of Christ. It teaches them the importance of personal effort making direct appeals to relatives, friends, and acquaintances (*Review and Herald,* January 21, 1873).

In 1886, the servant of the Lord observed this principle at work in Lausanne, Switzerland:

It is very hard to get any hold of the people. The only way that we find to be successful is in holding Bible readings, and in this way the interest is started with one or two or three; then these visit others and try to interest others, and thus the work moves slowly as it has done in Lausanne (*Evangelism,* p. 410).

Ellen White's description "then these visit others, and in this way interest is started" illustrates witnessing according to the way Jesus taught—a Christian will look for someone he knows and lead that person to Jesus.

There are many who need the ministration of loving Christian hearts. Many have gone down to ruin who might have been saved if their neighbors, common men and women, had put forth personal effort for them. Many are waiting to be personally addressed. In the very family, the neighborhood, the town, where we live, there is work for us to do as missionaries for Christ. If we are Christians, this work will be our delight. No sooner is one converted than there is born within him a desire to make known to others what a precious friend he has found in Jesus. The saving and sanctifying truth cannot be shut up in his heart (*Conflict and Courage,* p. 280).

But, how are we to fulfill the mission in a world that is so vast and varied if we are going to depend largely on personal witnessing? Was this type of outreach only appropriate for their times, when they had no access to the wonderful technology we now possess? Perhaps there is some logic here. But personal witnessing can still be surprisingly effective, capable of reaching people with extraordinary speed, much faster than most would suspect. Consider, for example, that while Andrew was looking for Peter, John was also looking for someone else to tell; then Peter headed out to tell Philip while both John and Andrew felt compelled to keep on telling other friends about their discovery. This means that the news was spreading not through addition, one here, another there, but instead by multiplication through successive levels of contacts—doubling repeatedly 2, 4, 8, 16, 32, 64—rapidly resulting in great crowds of people. Can you imagine how quickly earth's six billion human beings would be reached with this method? When we underestimate the possibilities, potential, and efficiency of personal witnessing, we make a serious mistake.

In churches where I offer seminars on soul winning, we hand out a questionnaire to the attendees to indicate what approach was most instrumental in their own acceptance of Jesus. Then, after the results are analyzed, all can more fully appreciate the potential of personal witnessing. You can do the same at your church; the results are always eye-opening. Expressed in percentages, here are the findings showing what motivates people to come to Jesus:

- Because a stranger knocked on your door, spoke to you about Jesus, and invited you to come to church: 1 percent
- Because you yourself studied or you enrolled your child in an Seventh-day Adventist school: 0.7 percent
- Because you listened to a radio program or watched a TV show that presented the Adventist message: 0.3 percent
- Because on your own and without being contacted personally by anyone, you came across a Seventh-day Adventist book, magazine, or flyer with message: 1.9 percent
- Because you attended an evangelistic series in response to radio, television, or print advertising: 0.6 percent
- Because you were born in the church: 29.1 percent
- Because a neighbor, friend, relative, or somebody at work or

school spoke to you about Jesus and invited you to church, or at least handed you some publication that contained the message: 66.4 percent

The results are very similar wherever I have conducted this survey. By no means does this play down the importance of our educational, radio, television, or publishing ministries. Absolutely not. The results of the publishing work, for example, are difficult to quantify. It is hard to fully calculate the effect of publications in the work of evangelization. Our data suggests that all of these instruments are worthwhile in support of the personal work carried out by the members of the church who are contacting others within their circles and leading them to Jesus.

Before Jesus ascended to heaven, He emphasized personal witnessing to His followers: "You will be My witnesses." A witness is someone who declares what he has personally observed or proved. That was the case among the first Christians. This is how the apostle John described it: "That which was from the beginning, which we have heard, which we have seen with our eyes, which we have looked upon, and our hands have handled, concerning the Word of life. . . . That which we have seen and heard we declare to you" (1 John 1:1–3).

Every Christian should be a witness to the love of Christ. Every Christian can begin a chain of witnessing that can grow exponentially. Every Christian can be a shining light that manifests the glory of God wherever he or she goes. Christ Himself has given us the example of how we are to work. By reading Matthew 4, we can learn the methods that Jesus, the Prince of life, used in His teaching:

And leaving Nazareth, He came and dwelt in Capernaum, which is by the sea, in the regions of Zebulun and Naphtali, that it might be fulfilled which was spoken by Isaiah the prophet, saying:

"The land of Zebulun and the land of Naphtali,
By the way of the sea, beyond the Jordan,
Galilee of the Gentiles:
The people who sat in darkness *have seen a great light,*
And upon those who sat in the region and shadow
   of death
Light has dawned" (Matthew 4:13–16, emphasis
   added).

"Light has dawned." What light? The glory of God was reflected in the lives of the disciples, and they, in turn, shared Jesus among those whom they knew.

We are to go forth to proclaim the goodness of God and to make plain His real character before the people. We are to reflect His glory. Have we done this in the past? Have we revealed the character of our Lord by precept and example? (*Faith and Works,* p. 61).

The world would have been evangelized already if we had followed the master plan of Jesus and if we had taken to heart the urgency of involving every church member in going to his or her friends, relatives, and neighbors. But, unfortunately, the divine plan has too frequently become just one more plan among many. This same pattern of viewing the divine plan as one among many was seen already in the late nineteenth century as we learn from this statement from Ellen White:

Every soul whom Christ has rescued is called to work in

His name for the saving of the lost. This work had been neglected in Israel. Is it not neglected today by those who profess to be Christ's followers? (*Christ's Object Lessons,* p. 191).

Think about that verb *neglect*. It doesn't mean "to reject," but rather, it implies considering something as of little importance, to take for granted, to suppose that everything is fine "as is." While carelessly neglecting the most successful method, some among us seem much concerned with coming up with new ways to carry out the mission—some "revolutionary" plan that takes little time, little money, and little effort yet is capable of swelling numbers at a phenomenal pace.

This book is not about promoting any such method. Instead, it is about preparing a people for the coming of Christ, for the edification of a glorious church without spot or wrinkle, a people who share Jesus at every opportunity.

The mission was not entrusted to us so we would reach the world for Jesus with a small groups of volunteers or teams of pastors and Bible workers, while leaving the majority of church members sitting on the sidelines. If the focus of evangelism was simply on getting the job done by any means, God Himself would have stepped in and completed the task, perhaps sending angels down to wrap things up speedily. He might simply have chosen to do this through talking donkeys or having stones shout out the good news along busy roadways.

God could have reached His object in saving sinners without our aid; but in order for us to develop a character like Christ's, we must share in His work. In order to enter into His joy— the joy of seeing souls redeemed by His sacrifice—we must participate in His labors for their redemption (*The Desire of Ages,* p. 142).

The great challenge that faces us is to help the church reflect the character of Jesus Christ. And to achieve that

> the greatest help that can be given our people is to teach them to work for God, and to depend on Him (*Testimonies,* vol. 7, p. 19).

What will Jesus have to do so that I, as a pastor or a member, will wake up to this reality? If for some reason I neglect Jesus' direct order and busy myself in useful work but not that which He specifically intended for preparing the church to meet Jesus at His return, what excuse will I proffer when He comes?

Questions to Consider

1. Does *evangelism* mean "swelling the numbers"?
2. What is the best method for growth? What method did Jesus teach us for carrying forward the gospel commission?
3. Secular businesses have very effective methods of marketing. Can we follow those methods too? Explain.
4. How did Andrew evangelize his world?
5. Are there people among our friends and family whom we would like to lead to Jesus?

Chapter 6

Friendship With a Purpose

João Apolinário led several people to Jesus during his lifetime. João now rests in the blessed hope of Jesus' return, but a heavenly crown awaits him on the resurrection morning. On one occasion, I was invited to lunch at his home, along with several of those whom he had led to Jesus' feet. The group was made up of businessmen, the sort one might take for successful secular individuals, indifferent about spiritual things. However, they seemed to have a wonderful experience in the Savior and were part of God's glorious church. João Apolinário had served as God's instrument for the purpose of bringing those persons to an understanding of the gospel. João was just being a Christian.

* * * * *

"What is Christianity?" asks Ellen White. And then she offers this answer:

[Christianity is] God's instrumentality for the conversion of the sinner. Jesus will call to account everyone who is not brought under His control, who does not demonstrate in his life the influence of the cross of Calvary. Christ should be uplifted by those whom He has redeemed by dying on the cross a death of shame. He who has felt the power of the grace of Christ has a story to tell (*Lift Him Up*, p. 230).

The problem is that many sincere Christians think that bringing people to Jesus means only giving Bible studies, knocking on the doors of strangers, or holding evangelistic meetings. Because they do not feel qualified to do these things, they become discouraged and live in a constant state of guilt and unhappiness. This chapter seeks to demonstrate that sharing Christ is a fascinating adventure, full of joy and unforgettable experiences.

If you want to lead souls to Jesus, you need first to understand that the work of conversion is divine and not human. You are only an instrument in God's service. He is the One who touches hearts, and it is the Spirit who convicts of sin. Therefore, if you want to have success in this calling, you need to pray.

Choose the person you want to lead to Jesus and then begin praying for him or her. Do that day by day and do not grow weary of this commitment. Two results will become clear. At the same time the Spirit is working in the heart of your chosen candidate, you will experience your own spiritual advancement. Prayer keeps you in communion with Jesus.

Next, be alert for divine guidance. Ellen White gives abundant counsel affirming that the mission of leading souls to Christ is simple and not at all complicated. Let's look at one example:

> The divine commission needs no reform. Christ's way of presenting truth cannot be improved upon. . . . Preserve the simplicity of godliness (*Evangelism*, p. 525).

I am deeply impressed by the words *simplicity* and *godliness*. No complications or sophistication are contemplated; the manner in which Jesus approached people was very simple. And it was successful. Do you suppose that in His time there were secular minds? You may label unbelief as you wish. There have been minds closed to the gospel always. This is not exclusive to our times. Jesus referred to the problem when He explained His use of parables:

> "Therefore I speak to them in parables, because seeing
> they do not see, and hearing they do not hear, nor do they
> understand. And in them the prophecy of Isaiah is ful-
> filled, which says:
>
> > " 'Hearing you will hear and shall not understand,
> > And seeing you will see and not perceive;
> > For the hearts of this people have grown dull.
> > Their ears are hard of hearing,
> > And their eyes they have closed,
> > Lest they should see with their eyes and hear with
> > their ears,
> > Lest they should understand with their hearts and
> > turn,
> > So that I should heal them' " (Matthew 13:13–15).

I ask you then, didn't those people described in Matthew
have hardened hearts and minds? Still, the Lord's evangelism
efforts met with success. Why is that so? In the first place, because He was the Gospel Incarnate; in the second place, because
He approached people in a way nobody seemed able to resist.
Just how did He go about doing that? Let's look at what Ellen
White says,

> Christ's method alone will give true success in reach-
> ing the people. The Saviour mingled with men as one
> who desired their good. He showed His sympathy for
> them, ministered to their needs, and won their confi-
> dence. Then He bade them, "Follow Me" (*The Ministry of
> Healing*, p. 143).

Let us analyze the five steps that Jesus followed as He led people to the kingdom:

1. He treated people as One who desired their good. The Lord didn't approach people as if He were merely interested in rushing them into church membership. No, He was genuinely interested in their well-being. Some Christians are so pushy when sharing their beliefs that relatives, friends, neighbors, or colleagues build "walls" to avoid them. They keep their defenses alert and their counterarguments ready. In some cases, they avoid the believer so they won't be trapped with a conversation topic that makes them uncomfortable.

Many now say, "If you want to be my friend, don't talk to me about religion or politics." If you accept the fact that we live in a secular society, why would you suppose that people are anxious to know your religious conviction? Nobody seems interested in this! And they would probably try to avoid any conversation with you.

Jesus didn't try to argue religion with people. Instead, He spoke to them about things that interested them. He related to people "as one who desired their good." Every human being wants to be treated like that. Who wouldn't want to listen to someone who talks with them about things they enjoy? And what interests people today? Usually sports, the economy, culture, and entertainment—just about anything other than religion. Well then, speak to them about their interests; don't mention Jesus and the Bible, much less your doctrinal beliefs. If you start talking about your religion, you will surely fail to win their friendship because your approach is all wrong.

Jesus said that we would become "fishers of men." Have you ever gone fishing? What bait do you put on the hook—chocolate? Perhaps popcorn? There's a good chance that you enjoy both of these treats, but fish aren't much into those flavors. What they are looking for are worms and juicy bugs, so that is the bait you offer them. That being the case, when you attempt to share Christ, why not apply this lesson?

Well, the next time you want to lead people to Jesus, do what the Master did. Don't start with religion; instead, talk to them about topics they are interested in. For example, if your neighbor is a football fan, try talking to him about football. Knowing that you are a believer, every time you come near him, he's probably getting ready for a religious "assault," but if you talk to him about his interests, he'll gladly be surprised.

If you want to bring a person to Jesus, try to become his friend. Remember that the words of a personal acquaintance are always more effective than those offered by a total stranger. Therefore, get close to people, talk to them about things they are interested in, find out what they like, familiarize yourself with their topics, and become fluent in them. Don't jump right in with an invitation to Bible studies and to attend your church. It's quite likely that they have no taste for such things yet. Take all the time that is needed to become friends. Accept invitations; spend time with them. Look at how Jesus treated people.

> When invited to a feast, Christ accepted the invitation, that He might, while sitting at the table, sow the seeds of truth in the hearts of those present. He knew that the seed thus sown would spring up and bring forth fruit. He knew that some of those sitting at meat with Him would afterward respond to His call, "Follow Me." Ours is the privilege of studying Christ's manner of teaching as He went from place to place, everywhere sowing the seeds of truth (*Evangelism*, p. 58).

Here's another illustration:

Jesus saw in every soul one to whom must be given the call to His kingdom. He reached the hearts of the people by going among them as one who desired their good. He sought them in the public streets, in private houses, on the boats, in the synagogue, by the shores of the lake, and at the marriage feast. He met them at their daily vocations, and manifested an interest in their secular affairs. He carried His instruction into the household, bringing families in their own homes under the influence of His divine presence. His strong personal sympathy helped to win hearts (*The Desire of Ages,* p. 151).

2. He showed them sympathy. This is the second step. Look at what Ellen White says,

My brethren and sisters, visit those who live near you, and by sympathy and kindness seek to reach their hearts. Be sure to work in a way that will remove prejudice instead of creating it. And remember that those who know the truth for this time and yet confine their efforts to their own churches, refusing to work for their unconverted neighbors, will be called to account for unfulfilled duties (*Testimonies,* vol. 9, pp. 34, 35).

This is divine counsel to keep in mind: *(a) visit the people who live near you; (b) try to reach their hearts through sympathy and kindness; and (c) disarm prejudice instead of creating it.*

Those are three fundamental steps. Dispel misconceptions; don't generate them. Instead, demonstrate a caring spirit and kindness. Nobody can resist the attraction of caring thoughtfulness. The other day I overheard someone say, "I don't know why I like to be around that young man; it's just that he is so nice." That's exactly the point: caring thoughtfulness attracts. If you want someone to listen to what you have to say about your faith in Jesus, first you have to win their appreciation for you as a person, because people will listen only to those who they like or admire. How does one become likable? Show concern, be kind, and be courteous. For example, learn their names; try to remember their birthdays and who their various family members are. They are your close neighbors, after all. Take them thoughtful little gifts on their special days. It will be well worth the effort. Say to your neighbor, "Happy birthday to your little girl! She turns six today; isn't that amazing?" How do you think your neighbor and that little child will feel— special, right? You didn't charge in with the Sabbath doctrine, the unhealthfulness of eating pork products, or the investigative judgment. You just went over to see your neighbors and showed them genuine thoughtfulness and affection, nothing more. When you do that, you are laying the groundwork that could lead those lovely neighbors to accept Jesus as their Lord and Savior.

3. He attended to their needs. This third step is very important. Human beings are motivated by needs. When a marketer wants to create demand for a product, he appeals to need, whether real or perceived. During the nineteenth century, the servant of the Lord wrote about this approach:

> In almost every community there are large numbers who do not listen to the preaching of God's word or attend any religious service. If they are reached by the gospel, it must be carried to their homes. Often the relief of their physical needs is the only avenue by which they can be approached (*The Ministry of Healing*, p. 144).

But people face more than physical needs. We must be prepared to consider their emotional needs as well. The world is full of sadness; unfortunate people have to deal with heartbreaking scenes in their homes, their marriages, with their children, etc. Many desperate people cannot sleep at night because they don't know what to do or where to turn for help. They are unaware of the solution found in Christ; they need someone to come close, be willing to listen, and lend a helping hand. Listening is key. Many people pay lots of money to have a psychotherapist listen to their woes. You must also listen and pay attention to their concerns. Let them know that you are a true friend they can count on.

4. *He won their confidence.* The key word is *confidence.* You don't put your confidence in someone you don't know. All too frequently we fail in our attempts to lead people to Jesus because we haven't won their confidence before presenting them with Jesus' invitation, "Follow Me." Once you have gained their confidence, you will see that hearts will no longer be hard. Rarely does anyone resist the love reflected in the life of a sincere child of God.

> In Christlike sympathy we should come close to men individually, and seek to awaken their interest in the great things of eternal life. Their hearts may be as hard as the beaten highway, and apparently it may be a useless effort to present the Saviour to them; but while logic may fail to move, and argument be powerless to convince, the love of Christ, revealed in personal ministry, may soften the stony heart, so that the seed of truth can take root (*Christ's Object Lessons,* p. 57).

To soften a stony heart, you have to invest time in order to develop a sincere friendship with this person. You will eventually gain his or her confidence.

5. *He said, "Follow Me."* How shall this invitation be made? On this point, we will need God's inspiration in answer to prayer.

Remember that we began this discussion about soul-winning techniques with the reminder that you must pray daily for the person you hope to lead to Jesus. That is true even when days turn into weeks, months, or even years. Don't become discouraged. God's timing is perfect. Even when it seems to you that nothing is happening, God is at work. Just keep on praying and cultivating your friendship with this person. One day, in the middle of an informal conversation, you say to your friend:

"Richard, there's something I've wanted to tell you for some time."

"What is it?" he replies.

"I have been praying for you daily during the past several weeks. I have asked God to protect and bless you, and not just you but also all your loved ones," you reveal.

"And why are you doing this?"

"Because you're a great neighbor, and I want to have you as my neighbor in the kingdom of heaven."

How do you think this person will feel when you make such a statement? We live in times when people hardly give a second thought about others; then, all of a sudden, here you are telling Richard that you are praying for him. Many of the people I have talked to who have done what I just described, report that their friends practically break down in tears from the emotion of it. They feel touched right down to the core of their being.

Now that you have taken the first step, press on.

"And there's more I want to tell you, Richard," you continue.

"What would that be?" he asks.

"You haven't been aware of it, but I have taken your name to my church prayer meetings on Wednesday nights. Even though they haven't met you, they are also praying for you."

"What?" Richard responds in surprise.

"In our prayer group, we pray for your wife and children, too, and for your hopes for the future."

Who could possibly resist such care and concern! Anyone, including unbelievers, will appreciate what you are doing. You haven't spoken to Richard about religion. You simply have enjoyed a friendship based on your sincere concern for him and his family. From time to time, you have lent him a helping hand, shown him kindness, and won his confidence; and now you tell him that as a special friend you have included him in your prayers.

Seeing how impressed he is, you now make the invitation.

"Say, would you like to join me this Wednesday evening at prayer meeting? Come meet some other friends who would love to get acquainted with you too," you offer.

What do you think he will do? There is a good chance he is going to accept, even if just to please you, because your friendship is important to him.

Right away you will want to contact the reception committee of your church. Every church should have a well-organized and efficient reception committee. Greeters are the face of the church. They should be thoughtful and friendly; they should smile sincerely and warmly; and they should know how to avoid being too pushy and yet not seem inattentive.

Give the head greeter a phone call and say to her: "Betty, look, this Wednesday evening I'm going to bring my friend Richard to prayer meeting. It's the first time he will attend our church, so please give him a special welcome."

On Wednesday evening, go by Richard's house and give him a ride to church. Of course you can't expect him to go alone. This is where your participation is crucial. You may not know how to give Bible studies or knock on strangers' doors, and you may not know how to preach evangelistic sermons, but you certainly can work for this person, step-by-step, by approaching him with loving interest, praying for him, and finally taking him to church.

As time goes by, you will see that interest in spiritual things will spring naturally from Richard's heart. When he starts asking you questions, that will be the moment to start offering him Christian reading materials. A book or a magazine can have an extremely positive impact. Godly publications have been able to open doors of steel. Sometimes, the piece of literature may lay forgotten for a while in a dark corner, but at the appropriate time, it will be read.

Few people can resist the drawing power of love. Love generates love. The method developed by Christ cannot fail. If you sincerely follow His example, you are going to have the same success He had, even when you find yourself up against seemingly stony hearts and secularized minds. The prophetic affirmation states that "Christ's method alone will give true success in reaching the people." Naturally, this declaration does not exclude other soul-winning activities of the church; it simply emphasizes the importance of working in the way Jesus did.

* * * * *

Let's return now to João Apolinário. He was wealthy and lived in a privileged area of São Paulo, Brazil, in an exclusive high-rise where apartments are priced at several million dollars. Only financially prosperous people could afford to live in that building. One day Arlete, João's lovely wife, stepped into the elevator and found a woman struggling to hold back her tears. She was the wife of another millionaire living in the same building. They were friends and for some time the Apolinários had been praying for this couple. They didn't speak about religion; they simply cultivated friendship, and on one pleasant occasion, they had all gone out to dinner at a very nice restaurant.

On that day, in the elevator, when she saw how sad her friend was, Arlete decided that the moment had come to attend to the emotional needs of this person. She invited the friend to her apartment. Then Arlete kindly suggested that her friend might consider joining with Arlete's friends who met regularly to give each other emotional support and to seek God's help in resolving their problems. What do you suppose the friend decided to do? She was going through serious marital problems and didn't know what to do. She loved her husband and by no means wanted their marriage to fail. If you are under the impression that wealthy secular people have no problems, think again. They also have children getting into drugs; they, too, are overwhelmed with problems.

That evening Arlete's friend came to the realization that she needed God in her life. The following week, she took her husband to the meeting; today, they both rejoice in the good news of the gospel.

But the story doesn't end there. The day I was invited to lunch at the Apolinário home at least six families were present; one had led the next; another had shared Jesus with yet others; and now they all formed part of the glorious church of God.

How did those rich, sophisticated families come to know the Savior? It was simply by following the witnessing model that Jesus taught.

Christ's method alone will give true success in reaching the people (*The Ministry of Healing*, p. 143).

Questions to Consider

1. How does God use our friendships in preaching the gospel?
2. How would you apply the five steps Jesus followed in leading people to His kingdom?
3. How can your church be organized so that those friendships cultivated by the members can be drawn into fellowship?
4. How can a decision for Christ be obtained from those you befriend?
5. Do you have a friend you would like to lead to Jesus?

Chapter 7

Why Should You Lead People to Jesus' Feet?

My greatest hero among evangelists, after Jesus, is the apostle Paul. I've studied his methods over and over again. It is amazing to analyze his way of getting close to people and how he composed sermons designed to penetrate deep into the hearts of those who listened to him. Paul's ability to dream helped him establish many churches. His dream was God's dream: to prepare a glorious church ready to meet Jesus at His return.

The day finally arrived when Paul, a prisoner in Rome, faced the executioner's sword, but his preaching continues on through the letters he wrote. I admire him greatly, and I will always be grateful for what he has taught me. Ellen White wrote about Paul as one who sought to build God's glorious church, without spot or wrinkle.

The apostle felt that he was to a large extent responsible for the spiritual welfare of those converted under his labors. His desire for them was that they might increase in a knowledge of the only true God, and Jesus Christ, whom He had sent. Often in his ministry he would meet with little companies of men and women who loved Jesus, and bow with them in prayer, asking God to teach them how to maintain a living connection with Him. Often he took counsel with them as to the best methods of giving to others the light of gospel truth. And often, when separated from those for whom he had thus labored, he pleaded with God to keep them from evil and help them to be earnest, active missionaries (*The Acts of the Apostles,* p. 262).

Notice Paul's concerns regarding those new Christians:

- "The apostle felt that he was to a large extent responsible for the spiritual welfare of those converted under his labors."
- "His desire for them was that they might increase in a knowledge of the only true God, and Jesus Christ, whom He had sent."

These two concerns had much to do with building up the glorious church of Jesus, and they led him to kneel in prayer with the new believers, asking God to teach them how to maintain a vital relationship with Him.

So then, how did they maintain that vital relationship?

- "Often he took counsel with them as to the best methods of giving to others the light of gospel truth."
- "And often, when separated from those for whom he had thus labored, he pleaded with God to keep them from evil and help them to be earnest, active missionaries."

Paul knew that Christians who don't pray, don't study the Bible, and don't share Jesus, do not grow. Such negligence places them on the dangerous path to self-destruction.

Ellen White also mentions that sharing Jesus is the secret to a successful and joyful Christian life. Let's take a look at the reasons why every Christian should become personally involved with the gospel mission.

1. A Christian who does not share Jesus is not converted. This statement may seem too radical, but it is a conclusion gleaned from the writings of Ellen White. Here are some of her words on the subject:

> The very first impulse of the renewed heart is to bring others also to the Saviour (*The Great Controversy*, p. 70).

This implies that if a person says he has been changed by Jesus and yet does nothing to share Him with others, something is missing— something doesn't fit. Such a one needs to review his Christian walk because,

> there is no such thing as a truly converted person living a helpless, useless life (*Christ's Object Lessons*, p. 280).

Notice the expression "truly converted." It is totally impossible to correlate true conversion with inactivity. True conversion generates in the heart of a Christian the desire to search for another soul to lead to Jesus' feet.

This is not a group activity to be carried out by the church. I cannot hide behind the pretext that my church is doing evangelism although I am only slightly involved. Sharing Jesus is a personal requirement.

> If the church members do not individually take hold of this work, then they show that they have no living connection with God (*Testimonies*, vol. 5, p. 462).

And what happens to church members who do not have a living connection with God? The answer is obvious. They may already be spiritually dead. They can be church members in good standing, complying with the standards, filling church offices, participating at potlucks, singing in the choir—but if they don't share Jesus, there is no living communion with Him. This is unnerving, because

> every true disciple is born into the kingdom of God as a missionary (*The Desire of Ages*, p. 195).

Anyone who is not personally committed to the gospel mission may look like a disciple, but he or she is not. He still hasn't been born into the kingdom of God. He is only a good church member, but without having experienced conversion.

2. A Christian who doesn't share Jesus will never reflect His character. The worst result of sin in human beings was to deface in them the character of God. Today, we are a grotesque imitation of God's character. We have become evil and selfish, and by nature, tend to pursue that which harms us. We've learned to pretend and to hide behind disguises. We can appear spiritually warm on the outside but cold in our souls. We are "a cake unturned" (Hosea 7:8), cooked on one side, raw on the other. Jesus called such persons "whitewashed tombs" (Matthew 23:27). Beautiful only on the outside—white marble and flowers—but inside filled with decay. But Jesus came to reproduce His character in our lives, to restore what had deteriorated, to bring us back to likeness with the Father. It is for that reason that He gave us the mission.

> God could have reached His object in saving sinners without our aid; but in order for us to develop a character like Christ's, we must share in His work (*The Desire of Ages*, p. 142).

This statement is clear. God has assigned to us the mission of sharing Jesus for this one reason: so that we can develop Christlike characters. If we don't participate in the Great Commission, it is impossible to achieve that ideal.

3. A Christian who does not share Jesus does not grow spiritually.
There is no such thing as a healthy Christian experience if there is
no growth. Of all life's stages, birth is the easiest. What do we
need in order to be born in Christ? It's just a matter of believing.
You could be in the deepest pit of sin, and if you called out to God
for mercy, Jesus would reach down with His mighty hand and receive you as His child. In that moment you are born into the
Christian life. That's all there is to it.

But to be saved, you have to do more than just be born; it is
necessary to remain saved and to grow. John says, "Beloved, now
we are children of God; and it has not yet been revealed what we
shall be, but we know that when He is revealed, we shall be like
Him, for we shall see Him as He is" (1 John 3:2). "It has not yet
been revealed what we shall be," states John. In this expression, the
idea of growth is implicit. It isn't enough to just be born into the
kingdom of God. Life is growth; the day you cease growing, you
die. The ultimate ideal is to reflect the likeness of the Creator. "We
know that when He is revealed, we shall be like Him, for we shall
see Him as He is." Ellen White echoes this thought:

> The only way to grow in grace is to be interestedly do-
> ing the very work Christ has enjoined upon us to do
> (*Christian Service*, p. 101).

Is it becoming clear? Some things happen without our aware-
ness, but if a Christian isn't committed to the task of leading souls
to Christ, then he or she will not grow. This phrase "the only way
to grow in grace" needs to be emphasized—it is key. To bring others to Jesus is not an assignment that I can squeeze into my spare
time. Either I do it, or I die. It is imperative. If I fail to do it, I will
remain a religious dwarf, as Ellen White phrases it.

Many, many, are approaching the day of God doing nothing, shunning responsibilities, and as the result they are religious dwarfs (*Review and Herald,* May 22, 1888).

4. A Christian who does not share Jesus is a Christian weakling. Every parent wishes to see his or her children grow strong and healthy. God also is a loving Parent, and He wants His children to be happy and growing in strength and vigor. For that purpose, He provided a strength-building routine:

> Well-organized work must be done in the church, that its members may understand how to impart the light to others and thus strengthen their own faith and increase their knowledge. As they impart that which they have received from God they will be confirmed in the faith. A working church is a living church (*Testimonies,* vol. 6, p. 435).

Note the progression in these thoughts. When Christians impart the light of the gospel to others, they strengthen their own faith and increase their own knowledge. Why is that so? The reason is that "as they impart that which they have received from God they will be confirmed in the faith." Notice the advantages that come from leading a person to Jesus' feet. You will increase your understanding. Every time you repeat truths to others you will be affirming them in yourself, and the questions raised by those with whom you study will lead you to study and dig ever deeper. But the benefits don't end there; truly your faith will grow stronger, and you will become firmly grounded in the truth.

What happens if you do not share your faith?

There is danger for those who do little or nothing for Christ. The grace of God will not long abide in the soul of him who, having great privileges and opportunities, remains silent (*Christian Service*, p. 89).

Are you beginning to see why some people start off on fire in their Christian experience but after a short while return to their previous lives? No long-term change occurred in their lives. These people opted to keep silent, and the grace of Christ did not long remain with them because they failed to share their faith with others.

It is those who, with love for God and their fellow men, are striving to help others that become established, strengthened, settled, in the truth (*Testimonies*, vol. 5, p. 393).

5. A person who does not share Jesus is vulnerable to apostasy or heresy. It is sad to see a Christian "die" in the first few years of his or her spiritual experience. Equally sad is to see a church member who, after years in the church, being blown away like a dry leaf by a dissident movement. The matter of apostasy is something that greatly perturbs denominational leaders. During my forty years of ministry, I have participated in many committees called for the purpose of solving the problem of apostasy. In many such meetings, I have heard emotional speeches arguing that new Christians abandon the church due to lack of preparation. That, however, is not the reason. In 1998, a study was conducted in the South American Division. We visited 328 individuals who had abandoned church membership, in 63 different locations, and asked them this question: "Why did you leave the church?" The responses were surprising.

- Disagreed with the doctrines   1.30 percent
- Joined dissident movements   3.90 percent

- Couldn't live up to the principles   18.8 percent
- Lacked friends in the congregation   76.62 percent

You can see that the reason was not due to lack of Bible knowledge. Knowledge is good, but it is not what keeps a Christian faithful. The basic problem is the lack of friendships in the church. New Christians are added to the church, but they are not included in the little "circles" of friendship that exist within the congregation. The new believers left their former friends but were unable to make new friendships within the church. After a short while, they grew discouraged and dropped out. You might ask what that has to do with sharing Jesus in order to lead people to Jesus' feet. It has a great deal to do with it. Notice the following statement by Ellen White:

> Christians who are constantly growing in earnestness, in zeal, in fervor, in love—such Christians never backslide. . . .
>
> It is those who are not engaged in this unselfish labor who have a sickly experience, and become worn out with struggling, doubting, murmuring, sinning, and repenting, until they lose all sense as to what constitutes genuine religion (*Christian Service,* p. 107).

Here, the inspired writer presents the work of sharing Jesus as the secret for not abandoning the ranks of the Lord's army. Everyone who makes the effort to share his or her faith will never apostatize, she says. But there is more. Ellen White goes on to say that Christians who live inactive lives, who do not become involved in leading others to Jesus, not only become discouraged but worse:

> they feel that they cannot go back to the world, and so

they hang on the skirts of Zion, having petty jealousies, envyings, disappointments, and remorse. They are full of fault finding, and feed upon the mistakes and errors of their brethren. They have only a hopeless, faithless, sunless experience in their religious life (*Christian Service,* p. 107).

Have you seen this sort of thing? Do you know someone who lives to criticize the church and its leaders? Ask them how many souls they have led to Jesus in the past year, and you will discover the reason for their negative behavior.

We often come in contact with sincere members who are very concerned about keeping up proper appearances. There's nothing bad about that. The problem is that if all their efforts are channeled in this direction and they forget that witnessing is the key to a Christian life, they run a terrible risk.

There are many who profess the name of Christ whose hearts are not engaged in His service. They have simply arrayed themselves in a profession of godliness, and by this very act they have made greater their condemnation, and have become more deceptive and more successful agents of Satan in the ruin of souls (*Christian Service,* p. 95).

When a Christian wishes to make only a profession of "piety," but does not become active in leading others to Christ, he or she runs the risk of deteriorating into an effective agent of Satan for the destruction of souls. This is truly shocking!

6. *A Christian who does not share Jesus will not participate in the promised revival.* God has a glorious dream for His church. He wants it to be alive, healthy, and holy for its encounter with the Redeemer. For this reason, He employs, among others, the tool of witnessing.

The church must be a working church if it would be a living church. It should not be content merely to hold its own ground against the opposing forces of sin and error, not be content to advance with dilatory step, but it should bear the yoke of Christ, and keep step with the Leader, gaining new recruits along the way (*Christian Service,* pp. 83, 84).

Revival is not about producing a church that upholds an elevated standard of behavior. Many sincere people worry about keeping "the world" from entering through the church doors. As we have just noted, the church "should not be content merely to hold its own ground against the opposing forces of sin and error." Instead, it must "keep step with the Leader, gaining new recruits along the way."

This is basic if we are seeking an authentic revival. Because, as Ellen White explains,

nothing will give bone and sinew to your piety like working to advance the cause you profess to love, instead of binding it (*Christian Service,* p. 98).

7. A Christian who does not share Jesus is not preparing for the coming of the King of kings. What is the right way to prepare for the coming of Jesus? Would that be by worrying about the date for the dreaded Sunday law or the beginning of persecution? Would it be by going out into the wilderness to study the Bible and pray like never before? Read what inspired counsel has to say.

Our faith at this time must not stop with an assent to, or belief in, the theory of the third angel's message. We must have the oil of the grace of Christ that will feed the lamp and cause the light of life to shine forth, showing the way to those who are in darkness (*Testimonies,* vol. 9, p. 155).

Prayer and daily study of the Word of God are indispensable, but these need to be accompanied by the work of pointing out the path to those who are in darkness. Otherwise, devotional life becomes empty and meaningless.

We are in the waiting time. But this period is not to be spent in abstract devotion. Waiting, watching, and vigilant working are to be combined (*Christian Service,* p. 85).

Abstract devotion is that which is limited to the study of the Bible and prayer. We need to include witnessing in the devotional life, and that means simply to seek others and lead them to Christ.

8. *A Christian who doesn't share Jesus will always be requiring attention and care.* There are many dissatisfied Christians with feeble faith. Ellen White again suggests the antidote:

This is the recipe that Christ has prescribed for the fainthearted, doubting, trembling soul. Let the sorrowful ones, who walk mournfully before the Lord, arise and help someone who needs help (*Testimonies,* vol. 6, p. 266).

A life without a mission is a life full of doubts. Do you remember what Jesus did when He saw that the disciples were burdened with doubts?

There is but one genuine cure for spiritual laziness, and that is work—working for souls who need your help (*Christian Service,* p. 107).

Ellen White tells a story that illustrates how helping others benefits oneself:

> I have read of a man who, journeying on a winter's day through deep drifts of snow, became benumbed by the cold, which was almost imperceptibly freezing his vital powers. He was nearly chilled to death, and was about to give up the struggle for life, when he heard the moans of a fellow-traveler, who was also perishing with cold. His sympathy was aroused, and he determined to rescue him. He chafed the ice-cold limbs of the unfortunate man, and after considerable effort raised him to his feet. As the sufferer could not stand, he bore him in sympathizing arms through the very drifts he had thought he could never get through alone.
>
> When he had carried his fellow-traveler to a place of safety, the truth flashed home to him that in saving his neighbor he had also saved himself. His earnest efforts to help another had quickened the blood that was freezing in his own veins, and sent a healthy warmth to the extremities of his body (*Gospel Workers,* pp. 198, 199).

I came to know Andy in one of the most violent cities of the world. He had a frightening reputation and had spent several years in prison paying for his crimes. While in prison, Andy came to know the Lord Jesus Christ. On a particularly bleak winter night, Andy felt that he wouldn't make it to the morning—his cell was freezing cold. In those conditions he heard me speaking over his cellmate's radio. That very night, the Spirit of God touched his heart. He had repeatedly heard people talk about Jesus, but he always thought religion was for sissies. He prided himself in being tough and went about heavily armed. Many people suffered from his criminal activity, which he had begun while still a juvenile. He blamed society for not providing him with a better path in life.

That night Andy felt that he was dying, and the thought frightened him. When things seemed to reach their lowest point, he came to understand that God loved him and wanted to give him a new heart. At once he begged God to do exactly that for him—to give him a second chance. Then he lost consciousness.

The next morning, Andy saw sunshine streaming through a window. He realized he was in the prison infirmary. "I was alive," he told me, unable to hide his emotion. "I hadn't died in the night. God really was giving me a second chance."

Some thirty years have passed since that memorable night in a freezing prison cell. Today, Andy is a living testimony of the transforming power of Christ. He is free and is doing an extraordinary job with an organization dedicated to helping rehabilitate juvenile delinquents. The last time I crossed paths with him, he introduced me to a large group of people that he had led to the feet of the Savior. "How could I keep quiet after all the Lord Jesus did for me?" was his smiling response to me when I asked whether he grew tired of sharing Jesus.

As Andy walked away, heading toward the auditorium, I stood there watching him in silence. He had discovered the secret of growth in Christ. He is part of the glorious church Jesus expects to find when He returns.

Questions to Consider

1. Do I hesitate at the idea of leading people to Jesus' feet? Am I timid and don't know how to begin? How can I learn?
2. List reasons why it is necessary to lead people to Jesus.
3. If not fear or a sense of duty, what other motivation should drive my desire to see others saved in the kingdom of Christ?
4. What relation does the love of God have on my salvation and that of others?

Chapter 8

What Is the Church's Purpose?

The book of Revelation contains many visions. There we find, among other things, God's dream for the future of gospel preaching. This is how the Lord introduced that dream to John: "After these things I saw another angel coming down from heaven, having great authority, and the earth was illuminated with his glory" (Revelation 18:1).

What a tremendous scene! The earth is illuminated with the angel's glory. Men and women, filled with the power of the Holy Spirit and transformed by the love of Jesus, light up the world with the glory of God. The character of Jesus is reflected in the lives of the believers; they are the light of the world. The forces of darkness quake in the presence of such splendor. The glory of the Lord, reflected by dedicated Christians, shines into every corner of the earth before the coming of Christ:

> Thus the substance of the second angel's message is again given to the world by that other angel who lightens the earth with his glory. These messages all blend in one, to come before the people in the closing days of this earth's history (*Selected Messages,* bk. 2, p. 116).

In order to live through this experience, the church must pass through a growth process; and to reach this ideal, God has assigned it the Great Commission. The church needs to understand that God wants His character to be reflected to the world through its members. They also need to understand that this mission of sharing Jesus is nothing less than a divine tool designed to achieve that revelation.

> Well-organized work must be done in the church, that its members may understand how to impart the light to others and thus strengthen their own faith and increase their knowledge. As they impart that which they have received from God they will be confirmed in the faith. A working church is a living church. We are built up as living stones, and every stone is to emit light. Every Christian is compared to a precious stone that catches the glory of God and reflects it (*Testimonies*, vol. 6, p. 435).

Notice what this quotation says about the importance of this mission in the life of the church:

- "A working church is a living church." The life of the church is related directly to its work.
- When the members share light with others, they "strengthen their own faith and increase their knowledge."
- While they impart what they have received, the members will be "confirmed in the faith."
- "Every Christian is compared to a precious stone that catches the glory of God and reflects it."

Once again we find the mutually beneficial cycle of the witnessing lifestyle. The members witness and bring others to Jesus' feet; at the same time, the witnessing strengthens their own faith and relationship with Jesus.

God has a purpose for the church, and the church has a reason for being. These two purposes are complementary. The fulfillment of her purpose helps the church achieve God's ideal. What is this divine purpose? Ellen White answers this question:

> The church of Christ on earth was organized for missionary purposes, and the Lord desires to see the entire church devising ways and means whereby high and low, rich and poor, may hear the message of truth (*Testimonies,* vol. 6, p. 29).

The church's energies should be directed toward this objective. Its work is indispensable if it is going to reflect the character of God and grow into the glorious community that Jesus expects to find when He returns.

> The church is God's appointed agency for the salvation of men. It was organized for service, and its mission is to carry the gospel to the world (*The Acts of the Apostles,* p. 9).

In the early years of the Adventist movement, the dream of mission was clear. In 1893, when the church was still in its first years of existence, the servant of the Lord declared,

> Our work is plainly laid down in the word of God. Christian is to be united to Christian, church to church, the human instrumentality co-operating with the divine, every agency to be subordinate to the Holy Spirit, and all to be combined in giving to the world the good tidings of the grace of God (*General Conference Daily Bulletin,* February 28, 1893).

History shows us that the Adventist movement was given a clear vision concerning the mission and the role of witnessing assigned to every believer. Unfortunately, the vision has changed over time. Many congregations at the present time seem to think that the church is a nursery for helpless infants who have been left without care and protection. At their first whimper, the pastor hurries to their side, warm baby bottle in hand. Many ministers are doing the work of babysitters. Their principal task is to soothe the "baby" so it won't cry. We forget that we as a people were born for a purpose, and we also forget that the best way to conserve the spiritual health of the members is to involve them in the work of sharing Jesus.

> Strength comes by exercise. All who put to use the ability which God has given them will have increased ability to devote to His service. Those who do nothing in the cause of God will fail to grow in grace and in the knowledge of the truth. A man who would lie down and refuse to exercise his limbs would soon lose all power to use them. Thus the Christian who will not exercise his God-given powers not only fails to grow up into Christ, but he loses the strength which he already has; he becomes a spiritual paralytic. It is those who, with love for God and their fellow men, are striving to help others that become established, strengthened, settled, in the truth (*Testimonies,* vol. 5, p. 393).

A spiritual paralytic! The figure employed by the servant of the Lord is blunt. A Christian who is inactive to such a degree will often find it easier to complain about everything.

> This is the recipe that Christ has prescribed for the faint-hearted, doubting, trembling soul. Let the sorrowful ones, who walk mournfully before the Lord, arise and

help someone who needs help (*Testimonies,* vol. 6, p. 266).

The mission to seek for sinners and lead them to Christ is not a task left to a few volunteers. At least, that should not be the case.

> The secret of our success in the work of God will be found in the harmonious working of our people. There must be concentrated action. Every member of the body of Christ must act his part in the cause of God, according to the ability that God has given him (*Review and Herald,* December 2, 1890).

Notice Ellen White's repeated use of the term *every.* The commission belongs to the church, but the church is composed of every member.

> Every man is to stand in his lot and place, thinking, speaking, and acting in harmony with the Spirit of God. Then, and not till then, will the work be a complete, symmetrical whole (*Testimonies,* vol. 6, p. 293).

In the church there is work for each one and all. In a sense, the mission of leading people to Christ is the duty of each one, but in another sense, it is the duty of all. The individual member who wishes to share Jesus will face many difficulties if he or she cannot count on the support of all the church.

In this context, the church's mission to evangelize cannot be carried out through evangelistic campaigns, but must logically be a permanent activity; it must be the normal life of the church. The missionary program of the church cannot depend on just one person. It is something that needs to be carried on every day. The doors of the church are open to receive the persons brought in by individual members. Everyone must see these persons as precious gems brought into the family of God, spiritual children who are being born into the Father's kingdom.

The church's missionary antennae must always be tuned to notice new people who are visiting. The arms and hearts of all should be wide open to receive them and to give them the care they need to grow and attain spiritual maturity.

Every church that is conscious of its missionary purpose should have certain ongoing programs.

1. An excellent reception committee. The greeters are the face of the church. They are there to receive visitors and make them feel welcome. The member who takes a friend to church for the first time should let the committee know in advance the name of the friend. In this way, when that person arrives, the greeter will be able to walk up to the visitor and address him or her by name. There is no sound sweeter than to hear one's own name mentioned. The visitor should be conducted graciously to a good seat in the sanctuary, and a Bible should be provided. This treatment gives an unstated message: "We gather here to study the Word of God."

2. Acceptance and friendship. The church and all its members should be educated to cultivate a climate of acceptance and friendship. The responsibility of making visitors feel loved and well received does not rest exclusively with the reception committee; it includes the entire church family. Every Christian who is born into the kingdom of God should be educated to greet visitors with friendly smiles. If anyone must be left out when greetings are given, let it be the friend or those who are already well acquainted, but the visitors must be given every reason to feel that they are in a warm, friendly place. When the visitors leave, they should carry with them a strong desire to return. This will happen naturally if the character of Jesus is reflected in the life of the church.

We are to reflect the character of Jesus. Everywhere, whether in the church, at our homes, or in social intercourse with our neighbors, we should let the lovely image of Jesus appear (*Signs of the Times,* August 18, 1887).

Every person who enters the church for the first time should see the beautiful image of Jesus in the face of each church member.

3. A fellowship lunch. Visitors should be invited to join the church family for lunch. At such occasions, all the members should warmly greet their newcomers and be sure to join them at the table. When visitors come alone, members should sit with them and include them in the conversation. Help the visitors feel comfortable and included. Many times attitudes are influenced more strongly by emotion than by logic. Some people who visit a church may not immediately understand the doctrines, but they will want to return because of the love they experienced there. For this reason, the church must practice loving others. In order to reach this goal, every Christian needs to pray daily, study the Bible regularly, and share Jesus.

4. An attractive prayer meeting. Prayer meetings need to be transformed into intercessory times. The entire church needs to pray for the persons its various members are working with. When the church of God prays, extraordinary things take place. I have seen miracles occur. When the church prayed, husbands who didn't want to have anything to do with Jesus, who beat their wives because of their faith, were touched by the Spirit. When the church prayed without ceasing, rebellious children returned to their homes and asked their parents to forgive them.

If every church member prays for the person he or she is trying to reach, and if the church will join in intercessory prayer for that person, rest assured that something out of the ordinary will happen.

Wednesday night meetings must include time for testimonies.

The members will have testimonies to share, telling the wonderful things God is doing in the lives of their friends. These should be worship times full of fervor and love.

5. A baptismal Bible class. This is another permanent resource offered by a mission-driven church. When believing Adventists lead people to Christ and the individuals begin asking questions about the Bible, the church should provide support so that those who do not know how to give Bible studies will have a place to take their friends. The members' only work at this stage is to accompany their friends to the class and sit beside them, helping them to look up the Bible texts. There will be a well-prepared teacher present who can take charge of teaching and explaining the points that perhaps the members cannot explain.

Churches that forget their reasons for existence end up becoming religious clubs. They meet once or twice a week to conduct a program, and nothing more. Think about the routine of such a church. During the week, the department leaders prepare their material for the Sabbath program. They distribute the responsibilities, organize the program itself, find people to do the special music, choose a few hymns, etc. Every day they make phone calls to remind participants about their parts in the program. When Sabbath comes, there they are, anxious that everything will turn out fine, and it usually does.

The program and the Sabbath come to an end, and they take a deep breath of relief and thank God that everything went well. But right away, they must begin the same weekly routine all over again; it's time to plan the program for the next Sabbath. Do you get the picture? The life of a church that has lost track of its purpose becomes nothing more than a series of programs. Just a few participate while the majority sit and watch. If they like what they see, they congratulate the leaders and return the following week; if they don't care for it, they criticize and perhaps look for some other church that offers better programs. This is an entertainment-driven church.

And what about the pastor? Unknowingly, he falls into the trap of preparing sermons of substance so that the church will be "well-fed." There's nothing wrong in preaching good sermons. The pastor is called to preach skillfully. But he needs to keep in mind that preaching is only a part of his pastoral duties. His mission is to prepare the glorious church for its encounter with Jesus. Too often, however, the pastor is far too busy preparing elaborate sermons for a church that is far too demanding. He has no time left over for anything else.

The servant of the Lord has counsel for such circumstances:

> If our ministers would preach short discourses, right to the point, and then educate the brethren and sisters to work, and lay the burden upon them, the ministers themselves would be saved from exhaustion, the people would gain spiritual strength by the effort put forth, and the result would be tenfold greater than now is seen (*Signs of the Times,* May 17, 1883).

Let's review these ideas:

• The minister should preach briefly and to the point.
• In addition to preaching, he should teach the members how to work.
• There will be a triple result: First, the minister will be saved from exhaustion. Second, the members will gain spiritual strength. Third, the results will be ten times greater than they presently are.

We need churches that have a clear concept of their reason for existing! This is the greatest need of the world: a people who know why they exist and understand God's reason for calling them upon the stage of prophetic history. Such people form a church with purpose.

Jesus states clearly what will happen to churches that lose sight of their purpose. On a certain occasion, He said, "You are the salt of the earth; but if the salt loses its flavor, how shall it be seasoned? It is then good for nothing but to be thrown out and trampled underfoot by men" (Matthew 5:13).

These words illustrate the church's reason for existence. Everything has a reason to exist but only if it fulfills its mission. The purpose of salt is to give flavor to food, but if the salt becomes flavorless, in Jesus' words: "It is then good for nothing but to be thrown out and trampled underfoot by men." And, what is the purpose of the church? It is to share the gospel. What is the destiny of a church that doesn't share the gospel? It might seem harsh, but Jesus doesn't mince words when He states what will happen.

The other day someone asked me, "How can we know if we are fulfilling our mission?" The servant of the Lord answers that question:

> The Thessalonian believers were true missionaries. Their hearts burned with zeal for their Saviour. . . . Hearts were won by the truths presented, and souls were added to the number of believers (*The Acts of the Apostles,* p. 256).

How do we know that the Thessalonians were true missionaries? We know that because "souls were added to the number of believers." Give emphasis to that word *added*. This is a reference to numbers. There is no better way to measure something than by counting up the numbers. If you tell me that you have lost some weight, I am naturally going to ask, "How many pounds?" If you tell me that you are growing old, I am going to wonder just how many years you have lived. Numbers may not be the best measurements, but so far nobody seems to have come up with anything better.

In the first years of Adventist history, the servant of the Lord wrote the following:

> Seventh-day Adventists are making progress, doubling their numbers, establishing missions, and unfurling the banner of truth in the dark places of the earth; and yet the work moves far more slowly than God would have it (*Review and Herald,* October 12, 1886).

How was it possible to know that those early Adventists were "making progress"? We conclude that indeed they were based on the fact that they were "doubling their numbers." On another occasion, Ellen White affirmed,

> If every Seventh-day Adventist had done the work laid upon him, the number of believers would now be much larger than it is (*Testimonies,* vol. 9, p. 25).

Well then, do you see how numbers were useful in tracing the history of the church? If the church fulfills the mission, the natural result will be numeric growth. The danger resides in becoming overly preoccupied with growing the numbers and forgetting that they have value only when they indicate natural results of true spiritual growth. As we already stated in a previous chapter, it is possible to grow numerically without growing spiritually, but it is impossible to grow spiritually without growing numerically.

Our priority must be the spiritual growth of the kingdom of God and the preparation of the glorious church that Jesus is coming to claim.

Questions to Consider

1. How does Revelation describe God's dream about how the gospel will be preached in the future?
2. How important is the gospel commission to the life of the church?
3. How did the gospel commission advance when the Seventh-day Adventist Church came into being?
4. What activities of the church aid in the fulfillment of the mission?

Chapter 9

Human Methods or the Master's Plan?

Church members aren't always clear what *evangelism* means. It seems that many confuse the mission with the method. The mission is to reflect the character of Jesus Christ in the midst of a world shrouded in darkness. In our time, humanity's duty to humbly give glory to God has been replaced by the desire to glorify self. Clearly, all believers should give thoughtful attention to the divine invitation:

Arise, shine;
For your light has come!
And the glory of the LORD is risen upon you.
For behold, the darkness shall cover the earth,
And deep darkness the people;
But the LORD will arise over you,
And His glory will be seen upon you.
The Gentiles shall come to your light,
And kings to the brightness of your rising
(Isaiah 60:1–3).

We live in a time of spiritual darkness. Humanism has pervaded modern thought and has profoundly influenced the spiritual realm. Today, some churches openly exalt human beings, but hidden behind the pretext of worshiping God. Glorifying men takes precedence over glorifying God. Human methods are given priority; and Jesus' master plan for evangelizing the world is seen as outdated. In this setting of spiritual shadows, the people of God are challenged to brighten the world with the glory of God.

The first angel appears on the stage of time announcing his message: "Fear God and give glory to Him, for the hour of His judgment has come" (Revelation 14:7). The glory of God must cover the earth before the coming of Christ. The entire universe must know that the glory once usurped from Jesus by the enemy still belongs exclusively to the Son of God. It is rightfully and exclusively bestowed on the King of kings and Lord of lords. Our God has on this earth a people called to proclaim the message of the glory of God both in theory and in practice—in theory, based on the Word, and in practice, expressed in sanctified character.

Considering this background, we must remember that God's great purpose behind the gospel commission is that His followers will more fully reflect the glory of God. In order to accomplish this goal, it is fundamental that every Christian become a shining light. Coming closer and closer to Jesus transforms Christians into ever-brighter lights. This process of drawing near to Jesus is not just theoretical; it is a real-life experience. There can be no communion with Jesus without daily prayer, without faithful Bible study, and without sharing Christ. It is necessary to repeat this concept time and again. The mission was not placed in human hands because God could not preach the gospel unaided by human agents, but to allow men and women to grow spiritually and come to reflect the glory of God.

This brings us back yet again to the principle of mutual benefit to both the person witnessing and the person he is leading to the Lord. Reflecting the glory of God is simultaneously cause and effect. The closer a Christian comes to Jesus, the more people will be led to the Lord; and as more people are led into a saving relationship with the Lord, the greater the reflection of Jesus' glory in the lives of those who are sharing Him. One action leads to the other;

one experience makes possible the other.

> As they [church members] impart that which they have received from God they will be confirmed in the faith (*Testimonies,* vol. 6, p. 435).

The challenge we leaders face is to guide each Christian to form part of the kingdom of God, to reflect the character of Jesus Christ, and to shine in the midst of darkness. By shining, we lead souls to Jesus. The servant of the Lord says that

> Christ's life is an example to all His followers, showing the duty of those who have learned the way of life to teach others what it means to believe in the word of God. . . . To every believer in Christ, words of hope have been given for those who sit in darkness: "The land of Zabulon, and the land of Nephthalim, by the way of the sea, beyond Jordan, Galilee of the Gentiles; the people which sat in darkness saw great light; and to them which sat in the region and shadow of death light is sprung up." Matthew 4:15, 16 (*Counsels on Health,* p. 387).

Notice these two clauses that appear in Isaiah's prophecy:

- "The people which sat in darkness saw great light."
- "To them which sat in the region and shadow of death light is sprung up."

According to the Bible, to preach the gospel is to demonstrate the glory of God to those who live in spiritual darkness. That was the way Jesus evangelized the world in His times. That is what the Father had in mind when He sent Jesus, and now our Lord says to us, "As the Father has sent Me, I also send you" (John 20:21).

Getting every Christian to reflect the character of Jesus and to lead others to Christ is not simply a question of methodology; it is the true cornerstone of evangelism. It is the foundation for real witnessing. All practical approaches and innovative methods must derive from that experience. Obviously, any method that leaves church members out of the picture must be considered as a false human invention.

Every time we forget or turn away from the instruction contained in the Word of God and in Ellen White's counsel, we find ourselves drinking from fountains of limited human wisdom. When we forget the divine instruction and try to imitate so-called contemporary methods that other churches use to achieve numerical growth, we find ourselves wandering down strange paths.

There's nothing wrong in observing the membership-growth strategies followed by other churches. All I am saying is that the Lord has given us sufficient instruction for completing the mission, and there is danger in applying human methods as the solution when we work in unproductive locations.

> The world has become a lazar house of sin, a mass of corruption. . . . We are not to practice its ways or follow its customs. . . . Christ said to His followers, "Let your light so shine before men, that they may see your good works, and glorify your Father which is in heaven." Matthew 5:16 (*Counsels on Health,* p. 592).

It is sad to notice how much money and time is sometimes spent conducting research and obtaining advice from secular business development experts when all those resources could be better channeled into studying how Jesus wants us to finish the work. Could it be that this is the reason we suffer constant frustrations and arrive at the mistaken conclusion that certain fields are too difficult to evangelize?

> If you would approach the people acceptably, humble your hearts before God, and learn His ways. We shall gain much instruction for our work from a study of Christ's methods of labor and His manner of meeting the people (*Evangelism*, p. 53).

How did Jesus approach people? Why did He have so much success in evangelism? How should we lead souls to Christ without making the work an impossible burden? This is the topic we will consider in the following chapter.

Questions to Consider

1. What is the difference between the mission and a simple method of evangelism?
2. Is my church just another community that exalts human beings?
3. What is the message of the first angel in Revelation 14:6?
4. How is the glory of God expressed in the lives of Adventist believers?
5. What do the two imperative verbs found in Isaiah 60:1 mean for the church?

Chapter 10
A Challenge to Pastors

After some hours staring at the surface of the lake, the frustrated king returned to his palace and scolded his wise old counselor.

"I couldn't see anything in the water. Stop your foolishness and tell me just who you thought I would discover to be my worst enemy."

"But, Majesty, it is hard to believe you didn't recognize him," answered the sage. "He was right there in front of your face. How could you not have realized that in the reflection of your own face lies the answer? You are your own worst enemy. You are a leader who wants only to lead but not to understand, yet you don't even know in which direction to lead your people. You possess an enormous army, but it will be of little service to you because, just like you, its officers are dominated by pride that doesn't allow them to see their own faults. You are harming yourself and your people—and this will lead to ruin. You are your own worst enemy."

This story has many variations. The apostle Paul referred to its message when he wrote, "See then that you walk circumspectly, not as fools but as wise. . . . Therefore do not be unwise, but understand what the will of the Lord is" (Ephesians 5:15–17).

"Walk circumspectly, not as fools but as wise" men. That's quite a challenge—especially for leaders. For Paul, the wisdom of a servant of God is related to understanding His sacred will. Have we understood the will of God as it relates to the Great Commission? How can I pastor my sheep if I don't know where we are going? How can I exercise a ministry or fulfill a mission when I don't understand God's will?

From God's perspective, the mission to share Jesus has been assigned to each church member.

> The humble, consecrated believer upon whom the Master of the vineyard places a burden for souls is to be given encouragement by the men upon whom the Lord has laid larger responsibilities. Those who stand as leaders in the church of God are to realize that the Saviour's commission is given to all who believe in His name (*The Acts of the Apostles,* p. 110).

Who is this "humble, consecrated believer"? It refers to every church member. God places this concern for soul winning upon him. Why? Because Christians need to grow spiritually so that they can eventually become part of the glorious church that Jesus wants to claim at His second coming. If I, as a minister, leave out church members in my outreach activities, I will demonstrate that I do not understand "the will of the Lord" regarding the gospel mission. If, in my eagerness to reach organizational goals and targets, I end up following methods that leave church members on the sidelines, I am ignoring God's instruction and condemning my "sheep" to perdition. God will surely judge me for this failure. I might have been sincere in what I did, but I did what God didn't ask me to do, and I forgot to prepare His glorious church, holy and without spot or wrinkle.

"The humble, consecrated believer," says the quote, must be encouraged by those "men upon whom the Lord has laid larger responsibilities." So who are these men? They are the ministers. The work of the minister is not to lead souls to Christ all on his own. It is God's plan that this work be carried out by the church member.

In laboring where there are already some in the faith, the minister should at first seek not so much to convert unbelievers, as to train the church-members for acceptable co-operation. Let him labor for them individually, endeavoring to arouse them to seek for a deeper experience themselves, and to work for others (*Gospel Workers,* p. 196).

The pastor must never do the work that God has assigned to church members:

Preaching is a small part of the work to be done for the salvation of souls. God's Spirit convicts sinners of the truth, and He places them in the arms of the church. The ministers may do their part, but they can never perform the work that the church should do (*Testimonies,* vol. 4, p. 69).

This message, directed to pastors, refers to preaching from the pulpit. It states that preaching is just "a small part of the work to be done for the salvation of souls." But it is God who does the work. How is that accomplished? It happens when He places souls in the arms of the church. The text concludes, "The ministers . . . can never perform the work that the church should do." It is hardly necessary to explain that "the church," is not referring to the institutional church but rather the church made up of individual believers.

The idea that the minister must carry all the burdens and do all the work is a great mistake. . . . That the burden may be distributed, an education must be given to the church (*Testimonies,* vol. 6, p. 435).

The work of the minister is to prepare, educate, teach, awaken, organize, inspire, and equip the church members so that they can fulfill their duty. They need to do this work because it is the means created by God to reproduce in them the character of Jesus Christ and to make them reflectors of His glory. The preacher must never think that his mission consists simply in preaching the gospel in any way he desires.

> God could have reached His object in saving sinners without our aid; but in order for us to develop a character like Christ's, we must share in His work (*The Desire of Ages*, p. 142).

Clearly then,

> the best help that ministers can give the members of our churches is not sermonizing, but planning work for them. Give each one something to do for others. Help all to see that as receivers of the grace of Christ they are under obligation to work for Him. And let all be taught how to work. . . . If set to work, the despondent will soon forget their despondency; the weak will become strong, the ignorant intelligent, and all will be prepared to present the truth as it is in Jesus (*Testimonies*, vol. 6, pp. 49, 50).

Do you see, then, how God's glorious church is to be formed? There will be no more weary, discouraged members. And why is that? Because the minister finally understands his duty and is now focusing on the mission. The minister understands that Jesus did not place the gospel work on church members because He needed human assistance; He assigns human beings the mission so they can grow and reflect God's character.

Ellen White is emphatic in her statement of this principle:

> Ministers should not do work that belongs to the laymen, thus wearying themselves, and preventing others from doing their duty. They should teach the members how to work in the church and community (*Review and Herald*, October 12, 1886).

By no means does God want pastors stepping in and doing the work that He has purposefully assigned to the church members. The church needs to grow; but if it doesn't commit to the mission, it will stagnate.

> Let ministers teach church-members that in order to grow in spirituality, they must carry the burden that the Lord has laid upon them—the burden of leading souls into the truth. Those who are not fulfilling their responsibility should be visited, prayed with, labored for. Do not lead the people to depend upon you as ministers; teach them rather that they are to use their talents in giving the truth to those around them. In thus working they will have the co-operation of heavenly angels, and will obtain an experience that will increase their faith, and give them a strong hold on God (*Gospel Workers*, p. 200).

From God's point of view, the responsibilities in fulfilling the mission are well defined. The church member needs to pray, study the Bible every day, and share Jesus. When he brings a person to Jesus, he will want to bring another and another. If he doesn't, he will eventually die. It is similar to a person eating but neglecting physical exercise; sooner or later, his health will suffer.

The pastor's work consists of teaching, educating, inspiring, challenging, enabling, and equipping the church members. In other words, he is to help prepare the church for its encounter with Jesus—to build the church of God's dreams, a church that is holy, glorious, without spot or wrinkle or any such thing. And this sort of work cannot be done from the pulpit. Some pastors have the misconception that giving a Sabbath-afternoon seminar for Bible instructors or holding a three-weekend series, training people to go out, two by two, is enough for the whole year. Not so!

Spiritual growth is a personal process, and it may take years. It is not something to be hurried through in an afternoon or even in a month. The kind of work Heaven expects in this line of service stretches over a lifetime. As we continue learning, we are constantly growing. It isn't enough to teach a few courageous souls who want to learn. The mission is not something for a select group of folks; it must include every member of the church. Every single one needs to be saved. Participation in the mission is the key to individual Christian growth; it is not an option. It is not simply an activity for those who have some spare time or feel they might have a gift for such. It is for every single member. This is why Ellen White stressed that

> those who are not fulfilling their responsibility should be visited, prayed with, labored for (*Gospel Workers,* p. 200).

This is the work of the pastor. He must visit those who are not involved in the gospel mission, spend time praying with and teaching them how to choose someone they personally know and can lead to Christ. This is the way to develop a strong church that will not easily fall prey to the attacks of the enemy.

> If our ministers would . . . educate the brethren and sisters to work, and lay the burden upon them . . . the people

would gain spiritual strength by the effort put forth, and the result would be tenfold greater than now is seen (*Signs of the Times*, May 17, 1883).

"The result would be tenfold greater." Isn't this what every minister would love to see? But this will never happen unless ministers come to understand God's plan for evangelizing the world, and then show willingness to follow the Lord's orders.

I know that the task is not easy. This is why,

Many pastors fail in not knowing how, or in not trying, to get the full membership of the church actively engaged (*Gospel Workers*, p. 198).

From the passage just quoted, pastors can fail in their ministry for two reasons: first, because they misunderstand their main function; and second, because even when they know what their duty is, they simply don't try to fulfill it. In which of these groups am I? Am I among those who never understood, or am I among those who do not accept? Do you remember what the wise counselor said to the king? "You are your own worst enemy." It isn't a question of circumstances, the territory, or the secular worldview of many. It isn't a problem of budget or other difficulties peculiar to the region. The problem lies in me. It is either because I don't know, or because, having understood, I have not tried.

And there's more. The previous quotation goes on to insist

if pastors would give more attention to getting and keeping their flock actively engaged at work, they would accomplish more good, have more time for study and religious visiting, and also avoid many causes of friction (*Gospel Workers*, p. 198).

If the pastors would give "more attention . . ." That term seems to indicate a third group is formed by those who understand their duty, who wish to fulfill it, but who simply fail to give attention. They apparently consider this to be just one more method among others. But that assumption simply isn't true. To get every member to participate in the blessing of leading a person to Christ is not merely about method. It is from this crucial process that everything else flows. Whatever method, whatever evangelizing venture that leaves the members on the sidelines is nothing more than human strategy. Of course, some of these endeavors may result in lots of baptisms, perhaps even increased tithe receipts, but in no way will those strategies fulfill the purpose God had in mind when He entrusted the gospel mission to the church as an instrument for spiritual growth.

"But pastor," one of my colleagues in the ministry said to me the other day, "if I wait for the church members to go out and find souls, the year will soon pass without any or few baptisms. Then what am I supposed to say to the conference leaders?"

This matter is more important than it might seem at first glance. It may even be connected to the qualifications of those elected to leadership positions in the church. Here's one more statement from Ellen White:

> Those who stand as leaders in the church of God are to realize that the Saviour's commission is given to all who believe in His name (*The Acts of the Apostles*, p. 110).

Do you grasp what God is saying through Ellen White? He is saying that before we elect someone to fill a leadership position in the church, at any denominational level, we must ask ourselves if this person *understands* that "the Savior's commission is given to all who believe in His name." Election to office is not about administrative talents, it is not about academic qualifications, it is not even about the positive résumé that outlines his career; but rather it has everything to do with this one question: does he or does he not understand the divine plan for the church?

Ellen White says this repeatedly and in a variety of ways:

> "I will rejoice in Jerusalem, and joy in My people," God declares through His servant Isaiah. Isaiah 65:19. These words will be proved true when those who are capable of standing in positions of responsibility let the light shine forth. . . . Christ's methods of labor are to become their methods, and they are to learn to practice the teachings of His word (*Counsels on Health*, p. 338).

Although those words were originally written for people in the medical work, it is dramatic to read this admonition from God's servant. She says that if I am capable of occupying a position of responsibility, I must not only let my light shine, but that, as a leader, I am under obligation to follow Christ's methods and to practice the teachings of His Word.

> The elders and those who have leading places in the church should give more thought to their plans for conducting the work. They should arrange matters so that every member of the church shall have a part to act, that none may lead an aimless life, but that all may accomplish what they can according to their several ability (*Review and Herald*, September 2, 1890).

The church will never advance beyond where I, as a pastor, will reach. It is my duty to take hold of God's dream and make it mine. I need to close my eyes and imagine the Lord Jesus Christ returning in the clouds of heaven, seeking His glorious church, without spot or wrinkle or any such thing.

Questions to Consider

1. Who might our own worst enemy be?
2. According to Ellen White, who is the "humble, consecrated believer"?
3. What is the work of the pastor?
4. According to *Gospel Workers,* page 198, what are two reasons why a pastor can fail?
5. What is the impact on my life of the quotation from *The Acts of the Apostles,* page 110?

Chapter 11

And Where Does That Leave Public Evangelism?

The remnant people came into the world with a birth certificate registered in the courts of heaven. Daniel 8:14 and Revelation 14:6–12 are the Bible texts that foretell the appearance on the prophetic stage of a faithful people, commissioned to preach the everlasting gospel.

When this took place, there were no organized churches or membership. How then could that handful of pioneers fulfill the gospel commission of going to the entire world and reflecting the glory of God? When Ellen White looked at the great cities where there was no Adventist church presence, she began pointing out the need to reach those people:

> The Lord has a message for our cities, and this message we are to proclaim in our camp meetings and by other public efforts and also through our publications (*Testimonies,* vol. 7, p. 115).

On another occasion, the servant of the Lord affirmed,

> The Lord desires us to proclaim the third angel's message with power in these cities. We cannot exercise this power ourselves. All we can do is to choose men of capability and urge them to go into these avenues of opportunity and there proclaim the message in the power of the Holy Spirit (*Evangelism,* p. 40).

Those "men of capability" were evangelists. Public evangelism consisted of a series of meetings conducted by experienced pastors. The gatherings were held in public halls, theaters, tents, or other public locales. The evangelist would arrive at the target city accompanied by a team of Bible instructors, and they would remain there, preaching for several weeks until a congregation had been established. This style of work was necessary in those times because there was no other way to establish an Adventist presence in those cities. But as soon as a church congregation came into being, no matter how small it might be, Ellen White would propose a different method of evangelism:

> In laboring where there are already some in the faith, the minister should at first seek not so much to convert unbelievers, as to train the church-members for acceptable co-operation. Let him labor for them individually, endeavoring to arouse them to seek for a deeper experience themselves, and to work for others (*Gospel Workers*, p. 196).

In these times, the work of public evangelism—as we call the series of meetings that often last up to two months and are led by an evangelist with a team of Bible workers—continues to be necessary in territories in which the gospel has not yet been heard. But in places where there are members, it would be wrong to leave the church members standing by as observers, and it could lead to divine reproof.

Instead, public evangelism must go hand in hand with the work performed by individual Christians. Consider the example of the apostle Paul:

> With Paul, personal work did not take the place of public evangelism, but was an indispensable companion to it

(*The Seventh-day Adventist Bible Commentary,* vol. 6, page 390).

In what sense do personal efforts and public evangelism work together? The mission of Christians is to lead people to Christ. It is Jesus who will transform them, and it is the Holy Spirit who will inspire in them the all-important decision. But it is the role of the pastor, as an evangelist and an instrument in the hands of the Spirit, to guide these people toward making their decisions. This is accomplished by means of preaching.

Perhaps we can compare today's evangelist to a midwife. He comes to assist the local church to give birth to new converts. What is sometimes called the "harvesting week" in reality is public evangelism with the participation of the church members. It is a week of many "births." But, in order for this to become a reality, the church needs to have been "pregnant" with people to whom the members have been witnessing. They would have worked personally with friends, neighbors, and relatives during a period of months. Then they lead these persons to the special week of evangelism so that the evangelist can help them take their stand for the Savior. In this way, personal effort and public evangelism continue hand in hand, as in apostolic times. This does not constitute some new method of work; it is the same master plan instituted by Jesus Christ to prepare the church of God's dreams.

If we follow the divine counsel for fulfilling the mission, we will never fail. The results will be positive. The church will be a living church; this will be seen by its growth, revealed in numbers and statistics. The problem with reaching large cities does not lie in the challenges posed by the conditions, but in the hardness of human hearts among those who refuse to follow divine guidelines.

Men make the work of advancing the truth tenfold harder

> than it really is, by seeking to take God's work out of His hands into their own finite hands. They think they must be constantly inventing something to make men do things which they suppose these persons ought to do (*Evangelism*, p. 117).

In the matter of evangelism, nothing more needs to be invented. Jesus would have been unfair had He given us the gospel commission without also laying out the way to fulfill it.

I have heard it said that the first time stamp vending machines were made available to the public, people would insert their money without reading the instructions. When no stamps popped out, they would become disgusted and start beating or kicking the machine. It wasn't very long until some machines stopped working. The post office would then have to repair those machines and then return them to service. Then, however, some postmasters added a sign written in large letters: "When you grow tired of trying everything else and the stamps still don't come out, try reading the instructions. Maybe that will help!" This story may be apocryphal. Nevertheless, regarding the church's mission, it might have helped had the Lord placed such a sign at the beginning of the Bible.

In 1898, Ellen White asked,

> Are we greater than our Lord? Was His way the right way? . . . We have not learned our lesson yet as we should. Christ declares, Take My yoke of restraint and obedience upon you, and ye shall find rest unto your souls. For My yoke is easy, and My burden is light (*Evangelism*, p. 58).

What is this yoke about which Jesus speaks? To what are we to be obedient? In the context, it clearly indicates that Ellen White is speaking about how God wants to teach us to carry on gospel work, preparing the glorious church of God.

* * * * *

As I conclude this chapter, it is night in Durham. I write under a soft light in my hotel room. Earlier this evening, I watched the bright eyes of many people who came forward during the altar call. Twenty, thirty, perhaps more, responded when I invited them to accept Jesus as their Lord and Savior. What really touched my heart was seeing church members come up front and hug the persons whom they had brought to the evangelistic series. This was God's wonderful people, getting ready to meet Jesus; this is the glorious church, without spot or wrinkle or any such thing. This is, without a doubt, the church of God's dreams.

Then I closed my eyes and imagined the emotion of the angels as they rejoiced. Read how Ellen White describes the angels' response.

> We are to be laborers together with the heavenly angels in presenting Jesus to the world. With almost impatient eagerness the angels wait for our co-operation; for man must be the channel to communicate with man. And when we give ourselves to Christ in wholehearted devotion, angels rejoice that they may speak through our voices to reveal God's love (*The Desire of Ages,* p. 297).

Questions to Consider

1. What purpose does public evangelism play in preaching the gospel?
2. In what sense does the work of the pastor and of the evangelist go hand in hand?
3. What is the term used by the author of this book to refer to an evangelist?
4. Of what yoke does Jesus speak, and what is its meaning?
5. Is it appropriate to try new methods of evangelism?

Chapter 12

Two by Two and in Small Groups

On Friday, the first one ever in Earth's history, Adam stood sad and alone in the lovely Garden of Eden. He had finished naming the animals and noticed the pairs: bucks and does, roosters and hens, and rams and ewes. *Why am I not part of a pair?* he wondered. God was nearby, waiting for Adam to speak up. When the Creator knew that Adam had realized his aloneness, He declared, "It is not good that man should be alone" (Genesis 2:18). So He put Adam to sleep, and created Eve.

When God says something "is not good," we can be absolutely certain that this is the case. God is never wrong. God's original plan to give Adam a companion was not just a question of physical compatibility. His social and emotional needs were also considered. Defense against the enemy was also easier with a partner. As long as Adam and Eve were together, the enemy would have a hard time tempting them into sin. On the other hand, if they separated, the odds were much better for the adversary to entice them to disobey God.

God's ideal is for humans to live connected to others. In that way they can lean on each other, make decisions together, and offer each other emotional support during difficult times.

When it came time to assign the gospel commission, a similar pattern was planned. Jesus had in mind this arrangement when He sent the disciples out two by two:

Calling the twelve about Him, Jesus bade them go out

two and two through the towns and villages. None were sent forth alone, but brother was associated with brother, friend with friend. Thus they could help and encourage each other, counseling and praying together, each one's strength supplementing the other's weakness. In the same manner He afterward sent forth the seventy. It was the Saviour's purpose that the messengers of the gospel should be associated in this way. In our own time evangelistic work would be far more successful if this example were more closely followed (*The Desire of Ages*, p. 350).

Let's review these points made by the servant of the Lord:

- Calling the Twelve, He *bade* them to go out two by two. It was not a suggestion or an invitation; it was an order.
- None of them was sent out alone. Brother went with brother, friend with friend.
- The purpose for this arrangement was so that they could "help and encourage each other, counseling and praying together, each one's strength supplementing the other's weakness."
- When the Seventy were sent out, He repeated the formula, sending them two by two.
- It was always Jesus' plan that "the messengers of the gospel should be associated in this way."
- In our days, the work of evangelizing would be "far more successful if this example were more closely followed."

Down through history, this example has often served as a guideline in forming missionary pairs. Church brothers and sisters often go out two by two to do missionary outreach on Sabbath afternoons. But the ideal Jesus envisioned was much more than just one afternoon of cooperation. Yes, missionary teams of two make sense when they carry out their labors during set periods of time. But God's idea of mission for His children is not so much a work assignment or a special method as it is a lifestyle. Preaching the gospel was not simply something to do if and when a person had some spare time available. The disciples were sent out to preach for the rest of their lives. To live was to witness; to witness was to live. They envisioned their lives totally wrapped up in proclaiming the gospel; while they went about their common daily tasks, they preached.

If we review the lifestyle of the disciples and of Christians in the early church, we will see that they journeyed through life two by two, not just to preach the message but always. Two disciples were sent to look for a donkey and its colt for Jesus' triumphal entry into Jerusalem (Matthew 21:1). Peter and John took care of the preparations for the Passover (Luke 22:8). Those same two went up together to the temple to worship (Acts 3:1). So clearly, the formation of pairs did not have as its sole purpose carrying out specific missionary tasks; it was about living the Christian life, helping each other mutually to grow.

> There is need of two working together; for one can encourage the other, and they can counsel, pray, and search the Bible together (*Evangelism*, p. 74).

Does a Christian need encouragement and counsel only when he or she is doing missionary outreach? We need encouragement and advice not just for preaching the message but also for facing life's many struggles. Therefore, every church that hopes to have spiritually robust members needs to organize itself into teams of two. This is not merely for the purpose of leading people to Christ; it also applies to living the daily life.

It might not be necessary for them to be together in every meeting; but they could labor in places ten, fifteen or even thirty miles apart—near enough together, however, so that if one came to a crisis in his labors, he could call on the other for assistance. They should also come together as often as possible for prayer and consultation (*Evangelism,* p. 73).

When we look at the lifestyle of our church members today, we recognize that we are far removed from the lifestyle and service God envisioned for His children.

Another matter of great importance is the organization of small groups within the church. Ellen White declares,

> The formation of small companies as a basis of Christian effort is a plan that has been presented before me by One who cannot err. If there is a large number in the church, let the members be formed into small companies, to work not only for the church members but for unbelievers also (*Evangelism,* p. 115).

In large churches people often do not know each other. That is a bit like what happens in large extended families—you know so-and-so is your cousin, but it doesn't really mean much to you. It is a sad reality, but in a church with seven hundred members, a member often ends up as a mere statistic. If some Sabbath someone doesn't show up at church, nobody notices and few seem to care.

It was never God's plan that His children would live concentrated in a single area. Big churches are generally the ones that evolve into club-style churches. The members are merely spectators of a program. How can you promote the active participation of seven hundred members all at the same time? The answer lies in small groups. That is an inspired answer. It was revealed by "One who cannot err."

And now the difficult question: how can church members be organized into small groups if the church can't even organize them into teams of two? Two is the smallest group. In order for small groups to function well, the pairs must function well first. A church that is organized in twos will easily form into small groups. If these groups work well, then most likely the entire church will function smoothly. And if the local church is succeeding in its mission, it will have a positive impact right up the ladder to the conference, the union, the division, and the General Conference.

Nobody was born to live in isolation. Why, then, should things be any different in the kingdom of God? Organize your church in teams of two. Don't leave any member to live his or her spiritual life alone. Living the Christian life is much easier when one has someone who takes an interest in—and prays for—him or her and when there is someone to pray for and team up with. The glorious church of God lives in this way!

Questions to Consider

1. How were the disciples grouped together when sent out to evangelize?
2. For what reason did the Lord send them out two by two?
3. Does the order given by Jesus to go out two by two have a wider significance for life?
4. What relation exists between this order given by Jesus and the statement by Solomon that two are better than one?
5. What is my responsibility toward those persons who are alone in church?

Chapter 13

Where Publications Fit In

I don't want to close this book without mentioning the importance of publications in the work of the glorious church that reflects the character of Jesus Christ. Printed material is of vital importance as believers head out onto the highways of life to share Jesus.

In 1857, the servant of the Lord had a dream:

> I dreamed that a young man of noble appearance came into the room where I was, immediately after I had been speaking. This same person has appeared before me in important dreams to instruct me from time to time during the past twenty-six years. Said he, . . .
>
> The press is a powerful means to move the minds and hearts of the people. And the men of this world seize the press, and make the most of every opportunity to get poisonous literature before the people. If men, under the influence of the spirit of the world, and of Satan, are earnest to circulate books, tracts, and papers of a corrupting nature, you should be more earnest to get reading matter of an elevating and saving character before the people (*The Review and Herald,* November 4, 1875).

Many years ago, this statement came to my attention, and it has been a consolation and an encouragement to me at times when I've lacked motivation to continue writing. I recognize that I am not a gifted writer; I am a minister who makes the effort to write. But I understand that

> our publications can go to places where meetings cannot be held. In such places the faithful evangelistic canvasser takes the place of the living preacher. By the canvassing work the truth is presented to thousands who otherwise would never hear it (*The Review and Herald,* October 7, 1902).

It's a thrill every time people come up to me and say that they came to know the gospel as a result of a book or an article I had written. I know that someday, walking down the golden streets of the new earth, I will meet many people who had never heard me preach but who had read one of the books I have written.

Obviously, publications would have little impact if it weren't for the wonderful people who distribute them among their friends, neighbors, fellow workers, and relatives. In the early years of our church's history, these people were known as colporteurs. Nearly every Christian was a colporteur back then. Today, literature evangelism for some is full-time employment—a lifework. Thousands of literature evangelists accept the divine challenge to serve as light bearers through the use of literature.

We need to keep in mind, however, that the publishing ministry involves more than full-time literature evangelists. A person doesn't necessarily have to be an official literature evangelist to distribute Christian publications. If every church member would distribute our publications wherever they live, the gospel would have been preached with greater efficiency and timeliness.

> There are many places in which the voice of the minister cannot be heard, places which can be reached only by

our publications—the books, papers, and tracts filled with the Bible truths that the people need. Our literature is to be distributed everywhere. The truth is to be sown beside all waters; for we know not which will prosper, this, or that. In our erring judgment we may think it unwise to give literature to the very ones who would accept the truth the most readily. We know not what may be the results of giving away a leaflet containing present truth (*Colporteur Ministry,* pp. 4, 5).

We don't know what result will come from reading a magazine or a book. Its message may seem to have been forgotten. Perhaps a book is left on a dusty shelf, its message ignored and useless. But that book could very well be a time bomb just waiting for its providential moment of impact! Only eternity will reveal the results.

In your personal outreach, once you have gained the confidence of the person you are befriending, take the initiative of sharing books and magazines. The written word will do its silent work at the person's convenience, perhaps answering questions that your friend may not yet have felt comfortable raising with you personally.

There is another possibility. You don't have to do full-time literature evangelism. I know many Christians who work their regular hours in businesses, factories, and other occupations, but during their free time they like to go out and distribute books and magazines. The result are very encouraging; they establish wonderful contacts with persons who might soon be brought to Jesus, they leave in receptive homes beneficial messages, and besides that, they may earn some needed income to help meet their families' needs if they choose to be part-time colporteurs.

When church members realize the importance of the

circulation of our literature, they will devote more time to this work. Papers, tracts, and books will be placed in the homes of the people, to preach the gospel in their several lines. . . . The church must give her attention to the canvassing work. This is one way in which she is to shine in the world. Then will she go forth "fair as the moon, clear as the sun, and terrible as an army with banners" (*Colporteur Ministry*, p. 7).

The world is in agony. Signs appear on all sides indicating that the second coming of Christ is near. It is time to return to our eternal home from which sin has long separated us. It is time to look up to heaven and see Jesus descending to Earth to receive His glorious church. Are you ready to go home with Him?

* * * * *

I complete this book in a hotel room this night in Durham. Looking out the window once again, I see hundreds of people heading home to rest after their workday. I'm filled with this assurance: He who began the good work will finish it. It gives me comfort to realize that the Spirit of God can do what human beings cannot. I have this hope that He will continue working in every human being who inhabits this planet.

Questions to Consider

1. What is the role of publications in the Lord's work?
2. How can I preach the gospel with a magazine or a book?
3. What advantage does the written text have over the spoken word?
4. Have you thought about sending a subscription of our church's missionary magazines to a friend or loved one?
5. Has this book inspired you to commit your life to God's mission? If so, when are you planning to start sharing Jesus with a friend or relative?

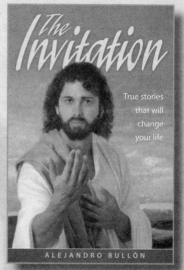

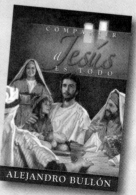
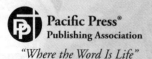